To Doctari

The "intrepid fisherman"

Happy christmas

Love Charlie & Tricia

CASTING
FAR & WIDE

*Dave Plummer holds an example of the huge fish
that can be caught across the seas*

CASTING FAR & WIDE

Compiled by

JOHN BAILEY

David & Charles

'But if one had the years of three Methusalahs looming ahead, there would still not be time enough to fish one half of all the rivers and seas that call so insistently.'

J. D. Greenway, *Fish, Fowl and Foreign Lands*
(FABER & FABER, 1950)

'I'm inclined to think that the love of sport and adventure is indicated, if existent at all, at a very early age.'

The Lure of Unknown Lands, Major F. G. Jackson
(G. BELL & SONS, 1935)

A DAVID & CHARLES BOOK

Copyright © John Bailey 1993

First published 1993

John Bailey has asserted his right to be identified as author of this work in accordance with the Copyright, Designs and Patents Act 1988.

All rights reserved. No part of this publication may be reproduced, stored in a retrieval system, or transmitted, in any form or by any means, electronic or mechanical, by photocopying, recording or otherwise, without prior permission in writing from the publisher.

A catalogue record for this book is available from the British Library.

ISBN 0 7153 9959 4

Book designed by Michael Head

Typeset by ABM Typographics Ltd, Hull and printed in Italy by Milanostampa SpA for David & Charles Brunel House Newton Abbot Devon

Contents

Introduction

My grandfather was a great and a keen fisherman who began his career in search of the pike, roach and tench of the Midlands. During the 1920s, however, his business of making sausage skins and gut for fishing lines began to succeed and his horizons were correspondingly extended. He began to travel for salmon in Scotland and for trout in the Alps, but most excitingly of all, he bought himself a boat and hired a skipper and went fishing for tunny in the North Sea. The gigantic tuna of this area captured the imagination of all anglers in the 1930s and grandfather was lucky enough to catch them to over 400lb. Sadly, on Christmas Eve, 1934 he died, only in his fifties and twenty years almost before I was born. Had he lived to open his Christmas presents that year, he would have received the *Where to Fish Guide*, a book that *The Field* has published for generations. That volume, which I inherited, now sixty years old and lovingly inscribed by my widowed grandmother, has always been near to me as a link with the angling relation whom I never knew. Perhaps grandfather is the reason that I took to fishing at such an early age with no encouragement from friends or family; perhaps his love of the sport was genetically passed on to me in some way.

Should you be fortunate enough to find a copy of that year's guide for yourself, turn to page 398. In my book, that page has been much decorated by the handwriting of my grandmother. Its title is simply 'Foreign Freshwater Fish' and beneath it it says:

> This list is admittedly tentative and incomplete and it only aims at giving the biggest specimens, most rod caught, of a few species recognised as important. But it may be of interest as indicating what has been and may be done in other lands.

The pen of my grandmother underneath simply adds 'Future plans for us?' She underlined several of the entries, one of which was the arapaima:

> The size to which this fish grows is uncertain, but it is acknowledged to be the biggest freshwater species in the world. It inhabits the Amazon and other great rivers of South America. The heaviest so far recorded for the rod is two hundred pounds, caught by Sir Walter Egerton on the Rupununi in September 1913.

Then there was the catfish:

> There are catfishes in most great river systems of the world, and it is uncertain how far they are related to each other, though it is obvious that they reach a great size. Uncertain what is the heaviest weight, but hundred pound specimens are well within expectation according to Dr Karl Heintz the noted German writer, and the Danube is said to yield fish of twice that weight.

Next came the goonch – 'A great catfish of India. One hundred and thirty-eight pounds, caught by Mr Van Cortland.' The dorado – 'The golden salmon of South America. A fine sporting fish with bad teeth.' Heavily underlined was the great lake trout and the next entry had a asterisk beside it. 'The Mahseer – a hundred and nineteen pounds. Caught by Colonel Rivett-Carnac on the Cauvery in 1919. For a long time India's most sporting fish was considered seldom to reach fifty pounds, but now there are several hundred-pounders on the record.' Next on grandmother's wanted list was the muskallunge:

> The great pike of Northern America. The biggest weight for a rod is fifty-eight pounds four ounces from Lake of the Woods, Ontario, caught by trolling an artificial minnow on July 2nd 1932. Specimens over seventy-five pounds have been caught in the past.

Then came Nile perch:

> Probably Africa's finest fish. One of two hundred and eighty pounds is on record from Lake No. Major Straker caught one of two hundred and a quarter pounds from Lake Albert in 1924. Another of one hundred and ninety-five pounds has been caught on rod at the junction of the Blue and White Niles.

The last underlining dealt with Africa – the tigerfish.

> Another very sporting African species with bad teeth. About fifty pounds seems to be the record for the rod so far, but the species is reported to reach at least a hundred pounds, especially in the Zambesi.

Grandfather's death changed all these plans. The tunny boat was sold, and grandmother did little travelling and no fishing until I was a small boy, when she went with me on the canals and ponds of the North. Here she helped me to learn my trade with bream or carp and, little by little, she helped me to prepare for more exotic travels. In a strange way, to some extent, I have tried to live out the dreams and hopes that my grandmother cherished for her departed husband. I personally have still not tasted a great deal of the fishing on that list. Indeed, there is more there than any working man can do in a lifetime. However, I have been lucky enough to sample months of travel and catch fish big enough perhaps to put a smile on my grandfather's face wherever he may be, should he be watching. On the species that I have not pursued, my researches have been exhaustive, preparations for adventures to come when money and time permit. I have read books, exchanged letters and made expensive telephone calls to all parts of the world at the dead of night to gather information of all sorts from all manner of people. What follows, then, in this book are the answers to those rough notes made by my grandmother sixty-odd years ago. The book aims to take the reader on those long-lost dreams, through the often hazardous journeys of men and women of today and yesteryear.

A part of this book is adventure angling and a great deal of bravery appears in its pages. For example, after eighteen-year-old Richard Slater had planned a trip to the Ganges headwaters he read a report in *The Independent* of three man-eating leopards at large in the very area he had targeted. To go seemed foolhardy, for over a hundred people had been killed in three years. He would be isolated and vulnerable in a tent on the river-bank. Despite the pleas of his parents and his own fears Richard went, caught mahseer and returned intact.

There is Shirley Deterding who flew a plane under the Ugandan radar screen in order to land on a prime stretch of the River Nile where she had heard that the perch were massive. Paul Boote spent nine months travelling around Asia on carts and local transport looking for mahseer and then went on to Africa where he suffered malaria and broken ribs. Johnny Jenson fished in the wilds of Greenland for char, feared that he had missed the boat back to civilisation and at one stage looked doomed to spend the winter on the freezing tundra.

Casting Far and Wide is, however, not simply a story book, for the logistics at the end of each chapter encourage anglers to leave their armchairs and to travel for themselves. This in itself is a heavy responsibility and any travelling angler must consider so many deeper issues than fishing alone. Should we, in fact, use the earth's resources to jet around the world for mere pleasure? Travel is a privilege and we must all treat it as such and cherish the lands and the people of whom we are, after all, uninvited guests. It should be unnecessary to talk about the problem of litter, but it is left in the most wonderful places on earth in horrifying quantities. Rusting cans, unburied faeces, fluttering pink-and-blue toilet-paper and the polythene bags once containing duty free goods that blow emptily on the wind are the trademarks of so many travelling Westerners.

Every travelling angler must respect not only the country he is visiting but also the people who live there. He must show respect for customs and for religious observances that might mean nothing to him personally. He must show politeness to all the strangers whom he will meet and take care with his dress, his jokes, his language and his behaviour. It is important to think carefully about the impact of all our actions in the wilder places of the world. What is the point of giving sweets to children when there is no dentist within a hundred miles? Far better are exercise books or ball–point pens, probably given to a schoolmaster or village elder for distribution to the children of the area.

Frequently the travelling angler will have to readjust his values and be far more flexible than he would ever have dreamed of being at home. He will have to be tolerant of local men fishing with nets, nightlines or even dynamite. He must realise that in some countries fish mean food and possible survival. The whole question of killing fish is brought to the fore: Western sporting ethics often dictate that pike, carp or even salmon and trout are returned to the water. In many areas of the Third World this is regarded as wasteful madness. Recently, Jim Tyree, the Norfolk angler, was lambasted in the British angling press for killing three very large Nile perch. What non–travelling Britains did not realise was that these fish went to feed poor villagers who were desperately in need of the protein they contained. I have had exactly the same experience on the Ganges when I realised that in everybody's best interest it was wise for me to give some small mahseer to the village. The people whom I had grown to love and trust simply could not understand why I was returning fish that they badly needed. The big mahseer went back, but many of the small ones went to the pot and perhaps to save a child. Indeed, fishing abroad makes the angler deeply aware of fundamental environmental issues. He sees threatening world problems at first hand and with any luck will come to care passionately about them and perhaps campaign against the worst atrocities that governments or industry seem intent on committing.

The travelling angler soon comes to learn a great deal about himself as well as the countries he visits and the fish that he pursues. He must learn to accept failure: foreign waters are often uncharted and the weather that affects them can be highly temperamental. Unpredictable monsoons, floods, droughts, migratory fish that fail to follow our timetables, local netting and unexpected debilitating illnesses can all ruin a fishing trip. All the travelling angler can do is to get there at the right time, at the right place, with the right tackle, but he must always accept that things so far from home can go wrong.

It is therefore essential to appreciate any and all of the fish that you catch. It is important not to expect enormous fish of every species but to savour every bite and every battle and every fish big or small. Hopefully, too, the travelling angler will learn to live every moment of his or her time away. It is not just the fish that make expeditions abroad so memorable: the heat (or the cold), the sunrises and sunsets, the mountains, the valleys, the birds, the animals, the buildings, the temples and, above all, the people, all make these the most special times of any angler's life.

So far, this introduction has been about the motivation of the book and about the theory. This is the armchair side of the work but there is also the practical information necessary for an angler to mount expeditions of his

A ferox rolls towards the net as the sun sets

own. Remember, if you are going to fish in a Third World or remote country, it is essential to take every single piece of tackle that you think might be necessary. Leave nothing to chance and take more than you think will be needed. If you run out of line or hook in most of the places mentioned in this book, there will be no chance of any replacement. Ensure also that the tackle arrives at the country of destination safely. There is nothing worse than getting to a remote lake or river only to find that rods have been broken in transit or that a pouch of reels has fallen out of the top of a rucksack. Always transport rods in the stoutest tubes possible and when you arrive at the check-in desk, emphasise their delicate nature to airline staff. Personally, I always like to keep the essential items of tackle and camera gear with me as hand-luggage on long flights. Clothes can always be bought in a local market, but the same is not true of vital specialised equipment.

Once a water has been reached, always listen to the advice of guides or locals first. This will win their respect and co-operation, but it is also virtually certain that they know more than you do about the area and its fish. After a while, try out your own ideas and techniques and if they are successful you will find that admiration for you grows. Always treat your guides fairly and generously. It should not be necessary to say this, but many Westerners expect guides to do the impossible and are angry with them if they cannot. Upon departure, remember that no gift is more valued than one of unwanted tackle. Lines, hooks, spinners and plugs are treated like gold dust in remote areas. I once left behind a cheap glass rod that was eventually sold to a local prince!

Always take with you a camera that you can trust implicitly, with new batteries, not forgetting those for the flash or motor-drive. If you estimate that you will need ten films, then take twenty and always be careful at remote airports that the X-ray machines are of the most modern type and will not fog the films as they pass through the security checks. If you are in any doubt, explain your problem to the airport security officials and try to carry the films through by hand. I generally take a wide lens, a standard lens and a telephoto lens. These should cover most situations, but remember that photographing local women, some shrines and virtually all military installations is at best impolite and at worst positively dangerous. I use Agfa transparency film of 100 ASA and generally I take at least half-a-dozen black-and-white films that capture the moodiness of cities and temples particularly well.

Good health is absolutely essential for a foreign fishing trip, so ensure that you receive all the necessary inoculations before you travel. Think carefully about diet in remote areas and take particular care with water or anything washed in it. Try to eat fruit that you can peel or anything that has been boiled or thoroughly cooked. If possible, watch the food being prepared and perhaps even clean your own plates and cutlery. Always drink boiled, purified or bottled water and take care not to swallow the water with which you brush your teeth. Keep your mouth shut when you are swimming, showering or in the bath. Take plenty of sun-cream and a sun-hat and avoid drinking alcohol during the heat of the day. Keep a careful eye open for snakes, scorpions and spiders. Should a big cat charge you, do not run but try to stand your ground. Also remember that some of the most 'cuddly' of animals are frequently the most dangerous. Elephants and hippos kill far more men than lions or tigers. My personal fear is of rabies and I feel that it makes sense to keep well clear of even the most adorable kittens or puppies around Third World villages.

Travel arrangements cannot be made too impeccably. If you are travelling by car, then have it serviced and take out insurance. When booking flights, hunt around for competitive fares, but remember that very often a few extra pounds or dollars spent can pay dividends in terms of comfort and length of journey. There is little point in arriving exhausted after a flight has taken you thousands of unnecessary miles around the globe. The same goes for hotels in many Second or Third World countries. There is little point economising if you lose out on sleep or if your health is affected or if there are problems about the security of your precious luggage. A decent hotel with a garden or pool may be just the tonic you need after a long period in the wilderness or after a particularly exhausting international flight. Getting through airports in Asia, Africa and South America can be a harrowing experience. It pays to keep cool and be polite and to follow all the rules implicitly. Officials can be alienated easily and they have the power to make your journey a nightmare. Ensure, therefore, that your passport, visas and all documents are prepared and accessible for inspection.

Good insurance for your luggage, especially your valuables, for your health and for your travel arrangements is very important and frequently I have had to call on it after a hazardous journey. Be careful with your money and keep it strapped with your passport, visas and air tickets in a money-belt. Traveller's cheques are universally accepted and the safest way to take cash around the globe, but you will need a certain amount of ready money. Dollars and sterling are popular almost everywhere, while Deutchmarks work wonders throughout eastern Europe and the Balkans.

I hope that this book will amuse and entertain, but it is also designed to inspire and inform. Before any trip, however, do check for absolutely up-to-date information and do not accept everything in the book as current. We live in a very volatile world and the rules are changing all the time. As I write (autumn 1992), Kashmir and Yugoslavia are out-of-bounds and who knows where the next axe may fall? It remains my ambition, however, that we may meet up sometime in the future by a splendid, isolated river and share a beer and many a story by the camp-fire. I am sure that as travelling anglers, we will have plenty to talk about the whole night through, until dawn pulls us back to the glowing waters and the fabled monsters beneath.

PART I

European Journeys

Ferox Trout

Fishing specifically for ferox trout, a great predatory fish that inhabits the largest, wildest, most inspiring of the Scottish lochs, began around the 1840s. John Colquhoun described a week on Loch Awe in 1842, in which 'trolling a giant trout is the very acme of rod fishing'. Certainly, he was more than fortunate during his week. On 30 April he landed an 8lb ferox; on 2 May he caught two fish of 6lb and 2½lb and on 3 May he landed a magnificent 9½-pounder. Colquhoun rose at 4am on 4 May and lost a big fish in mid-morning. However, a little later, after a forty-five minute struggle, he landed a 10lb fish. On 5 May, the last day, he landed a 2lb fish and as dusk began to fall he caught a beautiful 6lb ferox, of which he says, 'I have seldom taken out a more high mettled trout . . . The evening was bitterly cold so we did not bait again but pulled straight for the harbour and the next day left the loch.'

A few years later, Charles St John took up the quest for ferox in the Highlands.

> I was crossing Loch Ness alone one evening with my rod at the stern of the boat, with my trolling tackle on it trailing behind. Suddenly it was seized by a large trout and before I could do anything but take hold of my rod he had run out eighty yards of line and bent my still trolling rod like a willow, carrying half the rod under water. The loch was too deep for me and he snapped the line in an instant, the rod and the twenty yards of line which remained jerking back into the air, and sending the water in a shower of spray round. Comparing the strength of this fish with that of others which I have killed when trolling, he must have been a perfect water monster. Indeed I have little doubt that the immense depths of Loch Ness contain trout as large, if not larger, than are to be found in any other loch in Scotland.

By the 1880s, ferox trouting was established on the Victorian stage and Loch Awe continued as an important centre. Many of the regular fishers stayed at either the Loch Awe Hotel or the Taychreggan Hotel (where boats can still be hired and where ferox fishermen can still be accommodated in luxury). 1885 appears to have been one of the prime years for feroxing, when

(pages 14–15) Arthur Oglesby fly-fishing the Long Pool for salmon on the River Vosso at Bolstadoyri, Norway

The splendid, remote mountain setting of the ferox trout loch. Sometimes the Ice Age does not seem so far away. These great lochs can be up to twenty miles long, a mile wide and hundreds of feet deep

immense numbers of large trout were taken from the loch. Double-figure fish were considered almost average and all the guests confirmed that ferox trout far out-fought salmon, pound for pound. One of the lucky anglers was R. Macdonald Robertson.

A heavy squall was causing us to lose way when whirr went my reel: the water parted close to the boat, and a great big rosy-brown fellow leapt three or four feet into the air. Nichol (the boatman) had gained possession of my oar by this time and was straining every sinew to hold the boat. Which way would he go? Thank goodness he was off down-wind. Had he gone the other way Nichol could not have followed him: a few seconds run would have exhausted my short line. On we went, our friend steering an almost straight course for three quarters of a mile. On went the fish with never a check, utterly ignoring the two or three pounds pressure I steadily maintained, the bit fairly between his teeth. Then, apparently, our friend found the occupation of towing pall upon him and he straight away sounded and sulked. Nichol held the boat while I 'pumped' as strongly as I dared but without result. My antagonist lay sullen and motionless in the highest of dudgeons. Trying every means of civil persuasion in vain, I ultimately decided to bombard the perverse brute with stones until I could succeed in dislodging him. I told Nichol to edge the boat towards the shore, only five yards distant where we were able to gather a few large stones. Then pulling out again to windward of old ferox, we fired one missile after another. At the fourth discharge, his scaley majesty made a slight movement then rushed forth like a boy discharged from school and nearly emptied my reel before Nichol could get into his wake. And, if we might judge from the pace, he had fairly gained his second wind.

Now for the first time, I took a hurried glance to see how Nichol was standing the strain and when I saw his exhausted but game-to-the-last look, I longed to give him a dram from my flask, but this was impossible under existing circumstances. Nichol seemed to read my thoughts, for he exclaimed 'Dinna tak' your eyes off him. I'm doing fine!' The mad rushes now ceased and our good boat was steaming at half speed with an occasional slow down. As if to favour us, the wind lulled somewhat and

An Edwardian ferox held by the author in front of the loch from which it came

Shots of typical ferox scenery. The snow is still in evidence at 3,000ft even though these were taken in June

we could follow when it was necessary, upwind. It must have been at the end of three-quarters of an hour that I first brought the quarry to the surface where he came grudgingly, tugging, and the sight of us seemed to give him new life which it took some ten minutes to exhaust. During a quiet interval I said 'get the gaff handy Nichol'. No answer.   Then he replied 'No, Sir, I've left both the gaff and the net. I took everything out of the boat last night when I hauled her up out of the waves and must have forgotten to put them back. I remembered it all the moment you hooked him but I daren't tell you for fear it would upset you and spoil your hand, whereas if he broke away without you knowing the gaff was left behind I wouldn't have felt so bad. When he's not able to sit upright we'll slip the shore Sir.'

By this time the hardy warrior's strength was almost spent and as he came against the surface, lying on his side, the keen pleasure of seeing him almost ours was momentarily marred by observing him once more open his mouth and gasp heavily before he once more gave a sweep of his powerful tail and dived nearly to the bottom.

'He'll come now Sir,' said Nichol as he lay crouched at the water's edge and in he came, inch by inch, till he touched the stones. Lying on his handsome broadside, he allowed me to tow him gently towards Nichol who lay motionless. Almost before the stones were reached, Nichol's right hand was buried under the great spotted gills and the possessor of them was high and dry, struggling under Nichol's prostrate form.

That fish weighed 15½lb and I have seen the scales upon which it was weighed when I began my own ferox quests. For many years these were totally without any success at all, but one particular battle on Loch Quoich made me persevere. It was a wild, miserable day and in many ways I was stupid to be out in a boat on my own. After several hours' trolling around a particularly deep boulder-strewn area, my dead-bait was taken. I never felt a fish of this power before and the runs of the fish were deep and breathtaking, forcing me to follow into the swell. Soon I was motoring after the fish – trying to keep the line tight, trying to steer the boat and keep a proper speed behind him. I had not been able to reel in the two other outfits and one caught in the propeller. At times, the engine began to falter and I knew that if it should die there was no way that I could play the fish and work the oars in waters such as these.

Heaven knows how many times the line had dropped slack and all contact had been lost. Until it ripped tight, my heart could begin beating again. Finally, I was over the fish and rain was teeming down. There was almost as much water in the boat as without. My back ached but I was nearly there. I began to sense it. No fish, not even a ferox, could last so long against a 3lb test-curve rod and a 15lb line. I kneeled on the bench of the boat and pumped repeatedly, but the fish continued to dive and the line was lost to me. A little after midday, twenty minutes after I first hooked the fish, the rod suddenly fell slack in my hands and the ferox was away, free into the depths.

Until that ill-starred moment, ferox to me had been a fable, a legend, something out of history that I never expected to tangle with. Now, at last, I had, or at least made a start and my confidence began to rise.

It was not difficult to make the decision to carry on ferox fishing: the Highlands is a magnificent area and soon I began to regard the people in it as friends. There came a time when I could think of little but getting back north when I was working in England, and my heart would leap every time the car was loaded up with the mass of gear necessary for such an expedition and I would be nosing off into the night for the 500-mile journey. The snows, the squalls, the blizzards, the gales, the sleet, the sunshine, the flat calms, whatever the weather threw at me I laughed and loved it all. Feroxing was truly in my blood, coursing as strongly as it ever had done through the veins of St John or Colquhoun!

Ferox Investigation

The phone rang and the voice of an old friend asked if I would like to accompany him throughout the autumn to a remote Highland loch to research the habits of ferox trout. We were to be paid for our efforts. It was hardly surprising, then, that the next Sunday found me on the overnight train to Inverness, brooding over the years that I have pursued ferox trout. Converting the fantasy into fact has never been easy, but even my experience hardly prepared me for what was to follow.

Christopher, with best friend spaniel Maddy, met me at the station and during the long journey northwards outlined our task. We would be setting fyke nets over the burn mouths to try to catch ferox and salmon as they

A 'small' ferox has the spoon taken from its jaws

The boats lie idle on a dead calm day – surprisingly, often good ferox weather

Friend and dog concentrate hard

Trolling for ferox under blazing blue skies. Note the outriggers and depth finders and all the modern high-tech equipment

moved into their spawning burns. We would be electro-fishing those burns to establish the ratio of salmon parr to fingerling trout and we would put out gill nets to take char samples. Above all, we would be trolling big baits to try to take as many sample ferox as possible.

Scales would be taken from our ferox in the hope of establishing their age but, most vitally, we would be fitting them with radio trackers/transmitters so that we could follow them around the loch and up the burns. We had a dozen trackers, each with a different frequency signal, so that each fish could be identified. With luck, we would be able to plot ferox movements and perhaps even find where they spawned.

Around midday, we arrived in a Wester Ross village and from there we travelled up into the hills by Land-Rover. That rugged, beautiful journey took an hour, followed by a further two hours spent loading a boat with bedding, food, angling and scientific equipment and dog. We then faced a 6-mile journey down the loch to what I was told was the most remote inhabited bothy in Britain. Twenty-four hours after setting out from Norfolk, I at last saw our destination, utterly remote at the end of White Loch, dwarfed by towering mountains. We shared the bothy with some deer stalkers who, over a smoke-scented supper, advised us about our surroundings.

We awoke to typical weather, a force 8 gusting down the loch, bringing with it buckets of rain. Stupidly, men and dog went out and as we trolled we did at least try to avoid the spindrift zone. The gale was hitting the loch, driving the water like dust before a broom until it spiralled a hundred feet high in a wall of vapour. Sometimes we were caught: the boat shuddered, the rods leapt and Christopher and Maddy both disappeared in spray. For half a minute we would be utterly disorientated until the air cleared around the boat and the storm died back to gale force.

Yet that first day, in the evening, as the wind died a little, we hit into Enid. She fought splendidly with deep, long runs from the boat and showed herself as a lovely female fish. Her spots were huge, pulsating with life like fabulously coloured jellyfish with rings of fire. We boated her in a sieve to avoid net damage and laid her in a tray of tranquilliser. After forty-five seconds she was quiet. Then we unhooked, weighed and measured her and slipped the transmitter down her gullet with pipe and plunger. Her frequency number was 840. We took her to the beck by the bothy and kept her in a net overnight with stakes and wiring to fend off otters and pine martens. By the first of the next morning's light, we saw that she was alive, apparently unstressed and that the transmitter had not been regurgitated.

We released Enid into the Loch where she remained in the margins, dark against the stones, for two minutes before rocketing away into the depths. Half an hour later, we picked her up on the transceiver a quarter of a mile away, but the rest of the day we spent searching in vain.

Some fifty-five hours after release, Enid was tracked down three miles away from the bothy, having moved north-west to a group of islands. Fishing, though, had been patchy, possibly the result of quickly dropping air pressure. Indeed, we were in the middle of a four-day period without a take until the weather began to improve and the glass began to climb.

The only excitement was locating Enid again, twenty hours after her first recording. She had moved a further 1½ miles down the loch. This proved that she was surviving and it began to hint that ferox do not lurk territorially like river trout but that they roam far and wide. Perhaps they follow their prey, the shoals of char, or drift with the current.

Mercifully, reappearing sunshine saw us into ferox. A late afternoon bout of success saw us land six fish, two of which were large enough to take a transmitter. The ferox had suddenly switched on and in a spell of bright light and negligible wind the next morning the action was to continue. On our first troll we lost two big fish but wired up a further two good ferox for sound. Joy and Denis were now ferox frequencies to be followed and the nomadic picture that Enid had presented began to be reaffirmed by each new fish that we fitted with a transmitter.

Of course, one experiment with a handful of ferox on one loch does not prove anything conclusively. Possibly the stress of capture and of approaching spawning caused the fish to wander, but I doubt it. I am equally happy to stick my neck out and say that a rising or settled barometer is the prime time for the troller after big fish.

Towards the end of the period we began to lose plugs and spoons dangerously quickly and we were four hours from a tackle shop. We switched over to trolled dead-baits – 4-6in fish – and our results improved dramatically, both in numbers and size of ferox caught. A smelt, sardine, small herring or small roach seems to be at least as effective as a lump of plastic or metal and a fraction of the cost.

Perhaps the most important message of the White Loch is an environmental one, for it will be a long while before our ferox groundwork is fully scientifically verified. In the past, I have tended to troll public waters in Scotland thinking that waters 5-18 miles long could not be harmed by angling pressure. On these previous adventures north, I averaged one ferox approximately every fifteen trips out. On White Loch, this rose to 0.9 ferox per day, with many fish between 1lb and 4lb not included in the statistic. White Loch is private and it is possible that the fish were just less wary; however, I feel convinced that there were simply more trout.

It is a sad fact of life that vast numbers of trout are removed from open waters each season, although the amounts are ever dwindling. Nature just cannot keep repairing the damage being done and there is a serious need to begin conserving the wild brown trout on Scottish waters.

*A tagged ferox
is ready for release*

A large ferox which, unfortunately, died. In its throat could be seen the tail of its smaller prey. Later examination proved this to be a char

Ferox and Char
in Greenland

It is important to realise that the ferox trout is not simply a normal brown trout grown freakishly large. Rather, the ferox is a strain all to itself. This is what the Victorians believed and they have been proved correct by modern science. It seems certain now that ferox spawn only with ferox and their genetic characteristics are carried on, therefore, from generation to generation. The characteristics of the ferox, above all, are centred around

An ideal char morning as the sun begins to break up from the east

longevity. A normal brown trout peaks at around three or four years of age and dies at around six or seven years. A ferox trout, on the other hand, can grow for between fifteen and eighteen years, with a particularly fast growing period between seven and ten years. Obviously, this allows the ferox far greater room for growth, especially as by around three or four years of age the young ferox is almost totally predatorial.

The second key factor that accounts for the giant size of the true ferox trout is that the ferox only lives in lochs where there are adequate numbers of char to support a population. Char are shoal fish, and individuals generally average 4–10oz in weight. Their vast numbers and generally small size make them ideal fodder for the ferox which would be unable to prey successfully on individual small brown trout. This, of course, is why ferox trout are confined to alpine lakes: the char were trapped in them at the end of the last Ice Age when the ice retreated and they found themselves landlocked in the vast mountainous sheets of water.

In order to catch ferox, it is therefore important to understand the habits of their prey. Char are fascinating fish and in the lochs they have a definite lifestyle. In the early spring they mass in huge shoals, hundreds of thousands strong, often lying deep in the water. As the summer progresses the shoals break up and the char swim nearer the surface, sometimes taking small flies off the surface in the long summer nights. As autumn approaches, the char tend to mass together again and approach any incoming streams of water. Here, towards the end of the year, they spawn. The winter presumably is spent deep in the bowels of the loch until the following spring sees the cycle start again.

Although the average weight of Scottish and Irish char is around 8–16oz, in recent years huge char have appeared in Scotland. The British rod-caught record jumped swiftly from around 2lb to 4lb 14oz, to 5lb 7oz, to 5lb 10oz, to 6lb 1oz, to 6lb 7oz, to 7lb 1oz, to 7lb 7oz, to 8lb and now to an amazing 9lb 12oz. All this happened in a mere 5 years and is probably due to the effects of fish farming. Salmon cages on the big lochs must increase the fertility of the area in which they are situated. Pellets escape through the bottom and char grow more quickly. Also smolts of a few inches escape regularly and these apparently provide food for fast-growing char to grow into monsters.

Whatever the reason, hunting these big Scottish char is a fabulous business of excitement and beauty. The turn of September into October is probably the best time to hunt these fish as they leave the main body of the loch and look for the feeder in which to spawn. Big char swim in shoals into the fast streamy water to lay their eggs around the boulders and large pieces of gravel. Generally, the char seem to travel in during the late afternoon, move into the river at dusk, spend the nocturnal hours feeding and spawning and then travel back into the main loch some time after dawn. On a still night, it is possible to go down to the wide streamy runs and hear the char splash in enormous orgiastic groups: if there is a big moon, the water explodes into diamonds and silver. Fishing at these times can be good, especially as big males chase the small spinners from the area. My own blissful memories are

A mighty ferox indeed: the one-time British record brown trout of 19lb 9oz is held by the famous ferox man himself, John Hett (left) and the most marvellous host of all, Gordon Heath (right). The fact that larger ferox than this live in Scotland cannot be denied, and one day one of 25 or even 30lb is bound to be caught

of char caught in the pinks and lemons of a Scottish dawn.

I concentrate on 200yd of wide quick river that flow into the head of the loch. My spinner is a 2in Mepps with a piece of red cotton-wool tied to the end treble – this works, though God knows why. It is wise to cast far over the water and bring the little spinner back quickly. I give each area five casts and then move 5yd down-river, covering as much water as possible in these killing minutes before the sun is up and the day is truly begun.

Sometimes there are taps on the spinner and sometimes full-blooded tugs, all of which come to nothing and then, out of the growing blue, the rod is wrenched round, the reel screams and far away over the brightening water a 4lb body twists itself high in defiance. The males in their vivid scarlet waistcoats, spotted creamy white, are magnificent fellows; and the females, all pearly greys and blues and greens, are the most gracious of fish. But I do not keep more fish than I need: one for the table perhaps, but no more. Amazingly, even in a lock 10 or 20 miles long, these really big char might only number a couple of hundred. If they are caught at this vulnerable time as they gather to spawn, a sizable percentage of the leading char could be eliminated over a couple of weeks or even less.

What is fascinating is that due to their biological makeup, these char that have been landlocked for so many thousands of years still have the capacity

Travelling partner Joy holds a short-lived record char of 5lb 10oz

The desolate scenery of Greenland with the river twinkling in the distance

The full flow of the Greenland torrent

to grow large when their food opportunities change. The advent of salmon cages has awoken capacity for growth in them that has lain dormant ever since the last Ice Age. Not all char were marooned by the retreating ice and their cousins that live and feed in the sea and only visit fresh water to spawn can grow to a massive size. Arctic char have been caught around Canada, for example, that have approached 30lb in weight. Greenland, too, is a Mecca for the char fisherman, especially in the summer when the char leave the northern ocean to seek out the fresh glacial rivers of the world's largest island in which to spawn.

Johnny Jensen is a travelling Danish angler who was taken his rods over most of the globe. He describes below his experience in search of Greenland char in 1988:

After crossing a high plateau we finally got sight of the 'Waterfall Pool'. Excitement rocketed as I recalled the wonderful days I spent there in July 1985. There is a grassy area the size of a front lawn right to the pool and this campsite is fenced by an ancient fifteen foot stone wall which creates a very effective, often very necessary wind shelter. Unless the river decided to rise, this would be our truly perfect tent site. We charged down hill, half skidding, half running, threw off our backpacks, threw the gear onto the grass and rigged up our rods in seconds. Within two minutes Flemming was into a fish, the char for which we had travelled so far. The fight lasted no more than ten minutes but it was wild and furious as Flemming tried to control a fish that spent as much time in the air as in the water. Finally he managed to land it by hand with an ear-to-ear face-splitting smile all over his young features. Six pounds, a silver blue back with yellow dots, a green yellow vent with white-lined orange fins – a dynamite packed Arctic char! We photographed it against a blue, blue sky and then gently released it to the crystal pool. Soon we managed to land another brace of char of which we kept the biggest, a five-pounder, for dinner.

About an hour before sunset we finally took the time to erect the tent and get all our luggage packed in. Two rumbling stomachs prompted Flemming to start the fire at the base of the big stone wall, while I cleaned the fish, cut it into four pieces, salted them and wrapped them in silver foil. As soon as the flames were gone, we buried these four dishes into the hot embers. It was funny, but the first time I arrived at this river and discovered the 'Waterfall Pool', the fireplace with its metal grill was already in position. And funnily enough, three years on, this little Greenland stove was still in existence. And, as far as I know, it is still there now, lost in the wilderness, ready to be of service to any other anglers as crazy as us.

The fish tasted heavenly. This taste is something you couldn't even hope to catch at home with an oven. The firewood gives it that special taste of wilderness, of open sky and primitive camp life that can only be made with the outdoor bonfire. A hot cup of coffee in hand, we sat on each of our chosen stones and watched the wonderful colours of the sky set aflame as the sun sank behind the immense mountains opposite our tiny camp. We were the luckiest two friends on Earth that evening – until the Arctic fox in its black summer disguise found our plastic wastebag and spread its contents all over our site.

This is Greenland! The world's biggest island. In both '85 and '88, my destination was the Robinson River, thirty-five miles out in the field of Soendre Stroemfjord. This river is fairly narrow, but fierce and exciting. It springs from the icecaps' meltwater, snakes its way between rolling green hills and mountains, through huge cloudy lakes and finally runs into a huge bay on the southern side of the fjord. Its water is ice cold, not many degrees above freezing and this makes washing your hair a torture and bathing virtually impossible, unless you are a true Viking, of course. On the other hand, it would be impossible to find fresher drinking water that bubbles from the small springs. It is tasty, gin clear and available almost no matter where you decide to camp or hike.

Even though our campsite was a little paradise, we of course did some hiking in the mountains, watching birds, musk ox and other animals, collecting antlers, stones and flowers, resting where views take your breath away and always finding new pools to fish. Often, even after some knowledge of Greenland, it is possible to be deceived by the distances in such crystal clear air. A peak that looks only two miles away can take all day to reach and frequently Flemming and I looked at each other in disbelief and had to give up on some distant lake shimmering, tantalisingly in our sight.

My 1985 trip to Robinson River with my friend Kenth produced more fish than the second with Flemming. In the earlier trip we had several fish over six pounds and many between two and five pounds while Kenth got the biggest char on that last day of fishing that weighed just a fraction below eight pounds. This fish from the fjord looked almost like a sea-trout with a silver body and only very faint spots along its side. It is very interesting to see how the fish get increasingly more coloured the longer they have stayed in the river. They change from steel silver to blue silver and then to yellow and orange. Every night, the fish move from their holding spots behind rocks and migrate up-river through the many waterfalls. Each morning, therefore, you can count on a new batch of fish in your hot-spots. Even far upstream, and our camp is five miles from the fjord, we have caught silvery char that indicate that they have only been about one day in the river. Their travelling powers are amazing considering the waterfalls and thundering water that the Robinson River is all about.

Most of the char that I have caught on the Robinson River have fallen to light lures, spinners, spoons and small floating Rapala Wobblers – all between seven and eighteen grams. In the beginning, we used heavier lures to reach all the spots in the pool but after losing half our lures in two days we realised this wasn't a good idea. The char seemed to prefer the far bank and we had to cast over weeds that grow to within six inches of the surface. Heavy lures were replaced by light lures but they too disappeared into weed around rocks or were taken by fish that we could not control. On my first trip, with about five days to go, all I had left were a number of tiny spinners.

Fishing one of the lovely Greenland pools

I therefore invented the double and the triple spinner – small spinners joined by spring clips to produce a long, jointed, flashing lure. The first day I used this contraption I caught more than thirty-four pounds of char, which was double the normal catch rate.

In the fjord itself where the Robinson River flows out into the bay we caught a large number of Arctic cod called uvag. This cod is the most greedy fish I have ever seen. Out of ten casts you can count on hooking nine fish and it is possible to watch a school of ten to twenty fish follow open mouthed and fight over your lure. All you have to do is stop winding and it drops down into the big mouth of the nearest fish.

I've only the best memories of Greenland. The air, the water, the wildlife, the fishing and the camp life are all paradise. They add up to a perfectly peaceful, relaxing and most satisfying fishing holiday imaginable. I believe it is of immense psychological value to live in a natural balance with nature and to sleep, eat, rest, think and hike in a truly unspoilt environment . . . You go to sleep when you're tired and get up when you're refreshed. You eat when you are hungry and you walk in the mountains when you need to think and want some exercise. You fish when you feel like it without anybody to push you and with no pressing deadlines to meet. This might sound a little banal but for me it works. Everbody who's been to Greenland tends to agree and to say that they will definitely return.

Greenland fact file

Seasons

For char fishing in Greenland, I would recommend the period from mid-June to mid-August as the char migrate up the rivers in big numbers all through this period. It is said that you are most likely to catch the biggest number in June and July and the biggest individual fish in August. The weather can be changeable both in June and in August. A couple of anglers I know well went to bed in the evening after watching the sun go down and woke up the following morning to a white world outside the tent – in June! However, this doesn't happen very often. The days are normally quite warm when the sun is out but it does get cold at night, so a good, warm sleeping-bag is a necessity. During

A beautifully conditioned male char of over 6lb

this period you experience long daylight hours and the nights are no darker than a normal overcast afternoon. This is the best time of day to do your walking if you have to go far and to carry all your gear because it is refreshingly cool and often insect-free.

Luggage

I have found it crucial to be extremely selective on gear. Your backpack feels much heavier when you start walking in rough terrain and over swampy areas. There are many rolling rocks and you have to jump stones when crossing streams, so it is important to have at least one hand free for balance. It is better to break a hand if you have a bad fall than to get a broken or sprained ankle. You cannot walk back to civilisation on your hands and Greenland offers no roads or passers-by to offer rescue. That's the beauty of the place but it is also dangerous if you are careless.

Obviously, the boots you wear must be good, preferably with support for your ankles. For clothing, you needn't be too choosy, but it's a good idea to wear many layers rather than one or two so that you can take off some of them should you get too warm when you're walking. It is important to pack your waterproof clothes where you can get at them easily because the weather in the mountains can change rapidly. Pack all your gear in a plastic bag because you will be surprised how quickly a thunderstorm arrives overhead and explodes between the mountains. A sturdy, quickly erected tent is a necessity.

Food

Remember that you are in the wilderness totally alone. You have been dropped by boat or by helicopter and you will not see another person until that boat returns to rescue you, so it is important to bring enough food to last the whole trip. Obviously, you will top up with the fish you catch, but it is best not to depend upon piscatorial success for your complete survival. On both of my trips to Greenland, our foodstock consisted of black bread, cheese, salami, powdered soups, noodles, coffee, tea, cocoa, sugar, a lot of salt for the fish cooking, chocolate, and rum – for medical reasons, of course!

Health

Our medical bag consisted mainly of mosquito repellent, elastic support bandage and a whistle, in case we involuntarily got separated. We used the mosquito repellent for hands and neck but a mosquito net for our heads. Do not leave home without a net because the repellent works only for a limited period of time and when you start sweating becomes virtually ineffective. Fortunately, there is often a wind near the coast which moves the mosquitoes inland.

Travel Details

You can fly to Soendre Stroemfjord from Copenhagen only with Scandinavian Airlines System. There are departures at 10.15am on Mondays, Wednesdays, Thursdays and Fridays. The flight takes four-and-a-half hours. In the Soendre Stroemfjord the hotel is near the airport and there is also a camping ground where you are allowed to stay cheaply. Even if you are not staying at the hotel, you are allowed a free bath, which is very useful when you are returning from your trip. At the police office, right next to the airport building, you can obtain a fishing licence for the remote areas. You can buy these either by the year or by the month.

You can reach the Robinson either by boat or, if you can afford it, by helicopter. The 25-mile ride from the harbour takes about an hour by boat. The local residents are willing to take you to the river and pick you up again whenever you want for about £45 per person. The river offers fantastic fishing on almost all of its stretches. The best is in the bigger pools but definitely the most fun is to be found in the fast water. There is a 5-mile walk following the river to the first big lake and another 4 miles to the really enormous one called Taser Ssuag. The lakes contain masses of char and here all the fish are coloured in their most beautiful dress. Even though the water is very cloudy with sand from the glaciers, the fishing is excellent.

The Ferox of Europe

The glacial lakes of Switzerland, Germany, Austria and Italy are very similar to our own Scottish lochs but often on a grander scale. Fish life, too, appears to be very similar and in Europe there are huge cold-water trout that live for many years and grow to a great size by feeding predominantly on char. These, too, I believe we should call ferox. A big European ferox is truly massive: 30- and even 40-pounders are caught and there is always the chance that somewhere lurks a 50-pounder. Between 1931 and 1935 several very big fish were caught from large lakes in southern Europe – notably the Tranum Zee and the Lunzer Ste – weighing from 42lb to over 47lb. These were definitely very big brown trout and certainly not migratory fish.

One of the earliest British anglers to appreciate the fact of European ferox was G. D. Luard, who wrote of his experience in a post-war fishing book *Fishing: Fact or Fantasy*. In this engaging little book Luard talks about a journey that he took to Italy in 1912. The excitement started when he was staying on Lake Garda, where he met two fishermen arriving at his hotel to deliver a near-10lb lake trout for the guests. Not surprisingly, Luard was so impressed that he hired the men to take him out the next morning at dawn. Although they trolled patiently up and down the lake, they were unsuccessful that day. Luard was interested in the tackle that the Italian fishermen used: they pulled behind the boat a variety of small copper and silver spinners, some armed with hooks and some without. In all there were about twenty-five flashing pieces of metal attached to the main line and the attempt was to re-create a shoal of small fish that the ferox would hammer into and become ensnared. Some very big fish were landed in the Italian lakes in this way.

Unsuccessful at Lake Garda, Luard moved on to Lake Como where he had already booked rooms. Here, to his astonishment, appeared a master from his days at Harrow, with his wife and attractive teenage daughters. Luard and the teacher's family appear to have got on well that summer and made several excursions picnicking, sightseeing and sketching. They also made an excursion to fish on the lake and from here on it is probably better to let Luard's words speak for themselves.

On this particular evening then, we prepared to return across the lake in our habitually idle fashion. The weather was perfect, the sky a deep blue and the sun, now sinking a trifle, still a glorious gold. It was arranged that the two girls should row, the elder being stroke and the younger bow.

Older fishermen appreciated that Europe could give them enormous ferox trout. Here a retired major-general poses with a 17lb monster

I had asked them whether they minded loafing back by a circuitous route, as I'd brought my rod and tackle and would like to troll a minnow on the way, just on the chance of meeting one of the big trout.

It was a warm and pleasant evening and the others were not against the idea. So, the oarswomen being duly placed and the parents ensconced in the comfortable cushion seat at the stern, papa with tiller ropes in hand, I unmoored and stepping into the extreme bows pushed off with the foot and squatted down with the rod which I'd already mounted with a large silver minnow, a strong gut trace and a lot of lead, between my knees. The girls turned the boat and when we had progressed a little distance I made an overhead cast, well out behind into the side of the boat to avoid the oars. Then having gradually pulled off line till forty yards were out, I settled down to wait, without any serious expectation that anything would happen.

It was when our idle curving route had covered about a third of the distance across that I suddenly became aware that though not a breath of air was stirring, the boat was beginning to rise and fall on a slight swell, from the south.

I at once looked down towards the Como end, and what I saw gave me a serious shock, though I believe I did not allow it to show. Eight or nine miles away there was a thin white line on the water and in the sky over and behind it a big cloud as black as Erebus, and it was advancing rapidly towards us.

'Look,' I said to the others, 'I see there is a bit of a squall coming up the lake,' and to the girls, 'We'd better get on a bit quicker, if you can manage it. Never mind about me and my rod, that doesn't matter.' The girls answered easily and began to put their backs into it – luckily they were very competent rowers and they kept their heads. 'Not too hard,' I said, 'You've got a good way to go yet,' and they settled down to a steady stroke which carried us along well. Meanwhile the swell was increasing every moment and their father, who was more of a nervous type than their mother, suddenly said, 'I think we should face the oncoming waves, it would be safer.'

I'm afraid, although much younger than he, I was rather curt. 'No, there's only one thing to do – we must go with the swell and get behind the shelter from the promontory: if we went into the wind we should get on a lea shore where it is all rock.' Once he had had a look, he realised I was right, and we kept on at a good pace half before the wind. It was at this moment that a prolonged screech from my reel called attention to my almost forgotten rod. The girls hesitated in their stroke. 'Keep on steadily,' I said. 'Never mind the rod, if something breaks it must break.' In my heart I felt I was stuck on the bottom. But it couldn't be. Out here in the middle, the lake must be fathoms deep. It was a fish all right and a big one for he made a long curving run almost parallel with and in the same direction as the boat, so that I got in a certain amount of line. How thrilled I should have been under other circumstances! Now, however, my playing of the fish was virtually automatic – my serious attention was all on the darkening sky and that white line now drawing ominously nearer and bearing swiftly in its forefront a number of those great lumbering square sailed barges, which now race before the gale like yachts.

Wind too had begun to affect us a little, knocking the tops off the short waves as we rose and fell on them and sometimes spilling a little water on board. And all the while those two girls pulled steadily and pluckily on. Thank God we were well over half-way now – only one hundred and fifty yards and we would begin to feel the shelter from the long enveloping arm of

European ferox can be enormous: this monster weighed a staggering 34lb. Who is to say that similar fish do not exist in Scotland?

land on which the villa stood. I even began to have hopes that, if we once did get safely into shelter, I might yet play and land the great fish to which I was attached.

But it was not to be. After a period of docile following and short excursions, perhaps because the water was beginning to shoal, the trout suddenly made up his mind to be off once more to the deeps. A run, a leap half out of the water which showed me his size – about twenty pounds I guessed – and then a terrific run back the way we had come, combined with the speed at which we were travelling made the reel shriek. Obviously under such conditions one could not follow and, when virtually the whole of my one hundred and twenty yards of line had run out I held it hard with both hands to prevent a break at the reel. Nothing could stand that strain and there was a sort of deadened underwater kick on the line as something gave, deep down. I reeled in half the trace with the lead still attached. My minnow had gone but it was lucky I had not lost my line as well. By this time, even in the half shelter we had now reached, the short waves were choppy and rough and we shipped quite a lot of water but one hundred and fifty yards more saw us safe in the calm just as a terrific gust of wind descended upon us and the white wall of water with its flotilla of barges went racing by, looking magnificent now that we could watch them in the calm of security. A lucky escape indeed . . . for man and for fish both.

Ferox fact file

Seasons

Scottish ferox can be caught as early as mid-March right through to the end of the season in early October. However, chances improve considerably once the water has warmed up: 50°F (10°C) seems to be the critical point, some time around late April or May. May and June continue to be very good months but July and August see a decrease, generally, of ferox on the bank. September is again a good period and ferox seem to feed well until the October closing date.

This seems to be much the same case in Ireland, except that here the waters warm faster and late March and April can see very good results indeed. The high summer again can see a decline in sport until the autumn brings ferox on again.

March and April are the best ferox months in Europe, with sport tailing off badly in the high summer months as the water warms.

Dangers

By their very nature, ferox are fish of the hugest still waters. True ferox are only found in alpine lakes, which are generally at a high altitude and surrounded by mountains. In anything like a wind, this geographical situation makes all of them very difficult and dangerous to fish. Every precaution must be taken when afloat on these inland seas as storms can spring up fast out of nowhere and many of the waters give very little in the way of protection from a sudden gale. An added danger, especially on Irish loughs, is the possibility of hitting a sunken rock in a heavy swell. It is imperative, therefore, to know the nature of the water before going afloat. Never forget lifejackets, oars and rowlocks, no matter how reliable you think your engine is. Naturally, take plenty of fuel. It is also wise to tell some-body where you expect to be fishing on any particular day. If possible, fish at first against the wind. If, then, the engine breaks down later, at least you have the wind to help you back to your starting point. If you think there could be a danger of fog, a map and compass are useful aids. Always make sure that your outboard has a spare shear pin and that the boat has a bailer. Above all, never take risks of any sort as they can long be regretted.

Tackle

One of the most important aids for the modern ferox fisherman who is trolling at depth for a large predator is an echo-sounder. I use one of the more modern fish finders which not only charts the depth and the bottom contour but also shows up fish shoals and even large individual fish. I do not see this as cheating, as has been suggested. Without such a device it can take years even to know half of a water and even then what is actually happening beneath the surface will always remain a mystery. The fish finder is essential in pointing out immediately any drop-off, shallows or ridges and it will also find the shoals of char upon which the ferox feed. If you are very fortunate, it might also show up the big ferox, although these are nearly always on the move and the chance of catching one is slight. My own machine is a Humming Bird portable which I have had for several years and is very light and reliable. A pair of lantern batteries service it for around a week's hard usage and it has proved ideal in every way.

Rods and Line

Initially I favoured rods of between 2lb and 3lb test curve and around 12ft in length, but now I am not so sure and feel that shorter, lighter, more delicate rods might help the lure fisherman to detect takes more easily. Now, when fishing plugs and spoons I tend to use a 10-11ft rod of around 1¾lb test curve. Very often the plucks and tugs of a hesitant fish can be felt down the rod and appropriate action can be taken.

41

Once upon a time multipliers were considered the essential reel for the trolling angler, but now the bait-runner type reel is on the market and does all the jobs very well that the old multiplier used to do. My own trolling reels are Shimano 4500 bait-runners and over four years' hard usage they have always performed admirably. As a result, my multipliers have become virtually redundant for this type of fishing.

Once again, in my early ferox days, I tended to use 12–15lb line which now I have found is unnecessarily strong. In fact, 8–10lb line is generally sufficient for most ferox work, certainly in the British Isles. It is useful to load 80–100yd on to a spool and this can be changed every two or three days of hard work with little cost or effort. Putting a known amount of line on the spool is also useful in assessing how much line is in the water.

Bait

The question of plugs and spoons is an enormous one and now that the American market is opening up an extraordinary choice of deep-, middle- and surface-water lures is available. My advice is to buy a selection of deep-working lures, like Kwikfish plugs that can go down to around 30ft. I also have several shallower plugs for calm, clear days when the ferox tend to feed higher in the water. Silver and copper spoons, between 2 and 4in long, can also prove very successful. It is probably wise to consult one of the lure specialists who now operate in this country, as their range is enormous and they will give you all the advice needed.

The feasible alternative to using artificial lures is to troll a dead-bait. A small dead trout between 4 and 6in long armed with three trebles makes a superb, enticing bait that few ferox in the feeding mood can resist. Undoubtedly, there are days and waters where a natural bait easily outfishes the artificial and it is stupid to ignore them entirely. Naturally, make sure that the trebles used are needle sharp, as the fight of a ferox can be very long and take place at great depths, so the hook hold must be as secure as possible.

Accessories

The list of feroxing accessories is enormous. Vital is a good range of swivels and leads, together with a cushion to sit on for the long hours afloat. A couple of pairs of forceps are essential to take hooks out with as little damage as possible. Good boat rod-rests are an absolute boon but very hard to find. The best are imported from the USA and can be tracked down in some specialist tackle-shops. A landing-net will be needed, but do not attempt to keep a ferox for any length of time as the stress of capture is enormous on totally wild fish. Try to make sure that all the tackle is stowed away as neatly as possible in the boat, for, especially in times of heavy winds, it is vital that everything can be located easily and quickly, otherwise chaos can result.

Good waterproofs are essential for the frequent bad weather. For periods of calm, especially at dawn and dusk, it is wise to pack midge and insect repellent. Over the years I have found Jungle Formula to be as effective as anything on the market.

The European Carp Trail

This story properly begins with Lake Casein in southern France. This is a huge water comprising three arms set in arid landscape north of Cannes. Its history began slowly and only in the late Seventies and early Eighties did rumours begin to emerge from it. Along the carp-anglers' grape-vine, stories began to radiate of 50 and 60lb fish and soon the press began to carry photographs of enormous carp, held under blazing, Continental sunshine. Inevitably, the news got out and by the mid-Eighties the trickle of visitors south became a flood. Many of those travelling anglers were not successful, but those that were had the most incredible stories to tell. Phil Smith was one of those early anglers who travelled to the South of France and these are extracts from his story of his first trip to the legendary water.

Through midday and the afternoon we, as usual, lay around melting in the ninety degrees fahrenheit of blazing sunshine. A couple of points of interest are the tremendous displays of flowers at this time (the last week of May) though by September they tend to be tinder dry and dead. Another thing we noticed was the lack of wildlife. There were very few birds, no rabbits, squirrels or any of the usual things that can make a day's fishing here in Britain. We did see a few lizards, snakes and very large toads, which were at the very least different! On the afternoon in question it was Joe Taylor's turn at the rod and the three boilies on a dacron hair-rig were taken. The speed of the run was incredible and in no time there was a danger of losing all the line from the spool. We made for the boat, the clutch screaming as the fish tore off down the

An Eastern European style landing net

lake. The excitement was short-lived as we found the fish to be jammed solid almost forty yards out. From directly above the snag I heaved, wrapping the line around my arm in order to pull hard enough against the snag. Inch by inch, foot by foot and yard by yard I got the line back but there was no indication that there was a fish on the end.

With a slight breeze blowing down the lake, the boat was holding down-wind of the snag, so rowing back up-wind I pulled again and the line came free. Joe was now back in contact with the fish and what followed was exciting, even to me as a spectator. The fish kept deep, and here deep means deep, going down to sixty and even eighty feet. Imagine playing a fish to within fifteen feet of the boat, just out of sight directly beneath, when away she goes again on her powerful run vertically to the deeps! We yo-yoed up and down the lake, a hundred yards here and a hundred yards there, and all this time the fish was resisting heavy pressure put on by Joe. At last we drifted down the lake and there was still no sign of seeing the fish. After the best part of an hour, the fish finally broke surface and looked massive. When it finally slipped into the net, we were almost half a mile away from the original swim. The fish was not going to be tipped back now and with the greatest of care we made our way back to the bank. A crowd had collected to see the weighing which proved it to be fifty-four pounds!

Soon it was realised that other Continental waters might hold equally massive fish. Other pioneering anglers like Graham Cowderoy and Alistair Nicholson began to travel the Continent and they and others found big carp in a variety of countries. Holland, Denmark, Sweden, north and central France, Spain, Austria, Yugoslavia, Romania and Bulgaria all began to produce huge fish and show their potential. By the mid-Eighties it became obvious that just across the Channel the British angler would find waiting for him huge waters with huge fish that received little if any fishing pressure. In those days the Continental carp scene still belonged to the British angler, with very few of the locals appreciating the size of fish that swam in their waters. In many cases, even had they known of the carp available, local techniques and tackle were probably just not up to the task of landing such monsters from what are often dangerously snagged swims. Today, of course, the situation is somewhat different. Danish anglers in particular are very well organised and there are some superb French carp fishers. The Dutch have become very adept at picking up British carp-fishing methods and recently I found a Danish angler in the most remote area of northern Greece. British methods and baits have been widely copied throughout the Continent and not long ago I found roughly translated several chapters of my own book *Carp – Quest for the Queen* for sale in a kiosk in Slovenia!

The lure of foreign waters is very easy to understand. First, there is the weather. To fish under guaranteed blue skies is an event for the British angler and continuing balmy weather is ideal for the carp man who spends days, if not weeks, at the water-side. The lifestyle is also seductive: you can eat, drink, bathe and sleep when you want. Cheap local wines and exotic local foods all add to the glamour of a fishing session. But above all there is the promise of huge fish. In Britain a 20lb fish is considered big and a 30-pounder can still be the fish of a lifetime. However, in any decent European water 30-pounders are common, 40-pounders can be expected, and the sky is the limit. Moreover, the fish can be stunningly beautiful. Not all are hump-backed, deep-bellied wobbling monsters; many are streamlined and classically-scaled patterned mirrors. Then, of course, there are majestic common carp that are uncaught and absolutely flawless. Surely, one of these mint 40lb common carp must be the dream of any angler.

Any fisherman who travels with his carp rods on the Continent for long enough is bound to have some dramatic stories to tell. Sometimes things can be slow. Perhaps the weather has suddenly turned, or the fish cannot be located and the trip is dull and unproductive, but then there will be the occasions when everything comes right and catches of a lifetime seem virtually commonplace. Shocks, too, can be expected by the travelling carp angler. For example, Rod Hutchinson was asleep on the banks of Casein when his bait was taken early in the morning. A tremendous battle followed in the half light and his boat was towed, seemingly for ever, down the lake until an enormous catfish surfaced. No matter how he plotted it, there was no way that he could either get the mammoth creature into his boat or guide it to the bank, so reluctantly he had to cut the line and see the creature glide away from view. Everything has the potential to grow large in these warm, fertile Continental waters: huge catfish, grass carp, barbel, tench, pike, and even roach and bream are waiting there for the adventurous travelling angler.

To tackle these foreign waters successfully is a major operation and not to be undertaken lightly. The journey often involves a great deal of travelling, money and time and it is silly to go under-gunned and ill-prepared. The tackle must be up to the job in hand, if only to be fair on the fish. It is appalling to think of hooks and leads left in the mouths of these majestic creatures. Bait, obviously, is a vital consideration. In these inland seas, big shoals of enormous fish can consume frightening quantities of food and there is nothing worse than locating fish, tempting them down and not being able to hold them long enough to capitalise.

Above all, the key to unlocking these Continental waters is location. A boat and a fish finder are necessities. Despite the warm weather, fish are not always to be found near the surface and to stand any real chance of success the angler must know what is going on beneath. A portable Humming Bird is probably the favourite type of recorder. It is light, adaptable and reliable and shows up fish clearly as red dots above a black bottom contour. And what fish it can reveal! Some shapes have been known to be five dots long and as many as four dots deep. The mind boggles to think what these would be like on the hook and even on the bank.

A boat is also vital to take the angler around his prospective swim. Many of these large waters are reservoirs created over drowned farmland. Often there are sawn-off trees or even old buildings and obviously these provide sanctuary to the fleeing carp. It is imperative that the angler who has his sight set on 40lb-plus fish knows every inch of the swim where they are to be hooked. Without this knowledge, frequent disasters are inevitable.

Furthermore, it is highly likely that many battles will have to be conducted from a boat: the power of the first run of these Continental monster fish is often unbelievable and can empty a spool in seconds. Frequently, therefore, a boat is the only means possible of keeping in touch with such fish and, should they snag, it is simply irresponsible to pull mindlessly for a break. It is far better to get afloat, row over to where the fish is snagged and see there what can be done to relieve the pressure, land the fish and perhaps even prevent a carp death.

It is hardly surprising, then, that a European carp quest needs to be planned with almost military-like precision. The car, the tents, the tackle, the baits, the boat, the insurances, the money and all the other mass of considerations must be organised meticulously and checked off. The men who make these journeys frequently leave nothing to chance for they know nothing is worse than a breakdown or the absence of some absolutely vital piece of equipment.

The search for the first genuine, photographed and recorded 100lb European carp is well and truly on. There have been rumours that such a mighty fish has been stocked into Lake Casein, but as yet not one has come out. Almost certainly, somewhere such a fish must exist and it will probably be in one of the huge dams or pits that festoon southern and eastern Europe. But then, there are also the vast inland lakes that straggle through southern Germany and Austria to consider. It is impossible to guess what size fish lurk in these vast, underfished waters and only time will tell as more and more anglers make these almost heroic expeditions after bigger and bigger carp in the future.

There is, however, another side to European carp fishing. Not everything has to be on the massive, military operational scale. Take northern France, for example. The area around Tours is scattered with beautiful, smaller lakes, much like those we are used to in England. These are beautiful and gentle places to fish; they are intimate and full of features and there is no need here to cast heavy rigs to the horizon itself. The living and the fishing are both easy, but this does not mean that very large fish are not sometimes there to be caught. The 30-pounders certainly are, 40s probably and even bigger fish very likely. So, Europe offers carp fishing of all varieties to every level of carp angler and it will be many years yet before every water is tried, let alone thoroughly explored. In reality, we stand only at the beginning of modern carp exploration in Europe.

My own European carp exploits have not always been totally successful.

Famous Danish angler Johnny Jensen holds a superb grass carp – one of the species likely to be found in Europe

The first carp that I ever caught were in France in the mid-Sixties when I was there on a school exchange trip. A Mark IV carp rod and Mitchell reel were all the tackle that I could carry but I found them adequate to haul out a few nice fish from a magical lake in Tourraine. Although those fishing sessions were quarter of a century ago, I can still relive them in my mind's eye as they were so powerful and exotic: blistering hot weather, avenues of poplars, litres of cheap local red wine, a lost, lonely lake sweltering in the midst of wheat fields, heaving weed and bubbling carp and a rod bent constantly from dawn to dusk make up my memories of a truly golden time. I remember returning fish, to the consternation of the locals around that lake, and being offered 10 francs for a small, fully scaled common carp – 10 francs! It was a fortune to me then but my sporting ethics would not allow me to unbend and pocket the much-needed cash. The carp swam away free.

Even more powerful was an incident that occurred on a more recent trip to the Balkans in search of wild carp. It happened in the summer of 1990, after Joy and I had finished our fishing on the River Drau in Austria and sadly made our way across the high passes, southwards into what was then Yugoslavia. I say we left the Drau reluctantly: the fishing there had been absolutely superb and I had even landed a roach of 4lb 3oz, although there has been some doubt since as to its parentage. There were also barbel, chub, carp, pike, and even catfish. And all this could be found in a valley of colour, generosity, warmth, beauty and richness.

Slovenia, the first of the Yugoslav republics that we entered was, however, no let-down. It was every bit as lush as the Austria we had left but with more of a spice, less smugness and a real thrill of life going through it. There were the same dizzying mountains and lush plains scattered with rivers and whitewashed farmhouses, so we settled for a while at Bled, an enchanting tourist town built around a magnificent lake. The whole atmosphere was gaiety and excitement. I fished for rudd in the evening as the sun set behind the towering castle and as bands came out to play on the lakeside promenades. We would drink wine, bought from the waterfront café, and eat ice-cream at midnight once the fishing-rods were away.

I can't claim to have caught any big fish from Lake Bled: the rudd that I landed went to around 1lb and the chub weren't much larger. At night, though, as we enjoyed the music and wine and the spectacle of the floodlit castle, huge fish torpedoed out, glimmered a second in the lamplight, before crashing back into the clear water. Huge carp lived there and catfish, and, supposedly, great trout. After a week at Bled, the town was as hard to leave as Austria had been and it was with sadness that we drove off south into Bosnia.

The landscape became more arid and the weather even hotter. Tourists became fewer and GB car plates were soon non-existent. In fact, our car, which was loaded with tackle, became an object of wonder in the poorer, mountain regions. We discovered a large lake, lying alongside the Adriatic coast, which was slightly saline in quality. The carp fishing there was magnificent with wild, fully scaled fish reaching a possible 20lb. We took a little cottage close by the shores and fished there from breakfast-time to well past midnight. We lived on the beach, eating constant picnics of exotic local produce and drinking the rough local wine – sobering up almost immediately under the baking sun.

The former Yugoslavia has far more to offer than wild carp alone. On this journey, Joy and I heard of some huge carp living in enormous pits on the plains around Belgrade. We visited some of them but did not fish as time, by then, was growing short and we had several thousand miles to drive back home. The potential then, however, was virtually untouched, as I am sure it still is today.

One of our most dramatic encounters during a truly memorable stay was with a huge catfish. This I did not hook personally but saw attached to the line of a professional fisherwoman. For bait she used a live middle-sized carp hooked through the back and attached to an enormously heavy handline. A brick kept the carp tethered to the bottom in a well-known catfish hole.

The unfortunate bait was taken late at night and the handline hissed across the beach where we were sitting, drowsing, talking, drinking and eating under the stars. We rode after that catfish half the night and then we succeeded in bringing it to the surface as dawn finally approached. It is pointless to talk about the size of that fish, for I would not be believed. At that time, however, it was the largest fish I had ever seen and I realised that it was far too large to bring into the boat. It began to crash on the surface and the fisherwoman's husband swiftly cut the handline with his knife and in a final swirl the catfish was lost to us all. At the time I was furious that such a prize was lost and only now can I see the sense in what was done.

Since the happy days of my trip to Yugoslavia, the news from that war-torn country has been appalling. As I write now, in autumn 1992, return would be impossible and I wonder if I will ever fish that country again for its extraordinary carp.

There is no doubt that the Balkans hold some exceptional fish, and wherever Joy and I went we heard rumours of monsters, lost, seen or even, occasionally, caught. One rumour, however, has so many facts and names to it that it must be true. The Danube winds its massive way from west to east, separating Romania from Bulgaria until it turns north and forms a great delta into the Black Sea. Just into fresh water, on the 19 October 1983, a German, Wolfgang Krischke, found himself playing an unforgettable catfish that was so large that it kept him and his family straining in battle for more than three-and-a-half hours.

It all started at about 5pm when Krischke's group decided to start fishing. They were live-baiting with 6in carp on large sea hooks in an area where a very large swirl had showed there was some predatory activity. A little after five, a 10lb catfish was landed and there was a certain amount of discussion about whether to move on or to stay in the swim. During the debate a man was heard calling, shouting for help, saying that he had hooked a big fish. It was Josef Krischke, Wolfgang's father. Josef played the unseen fish for around ten minutes before deciding that it was too much for him to handle. He had already suffered two heart attacks and wisely decided to pass the rod

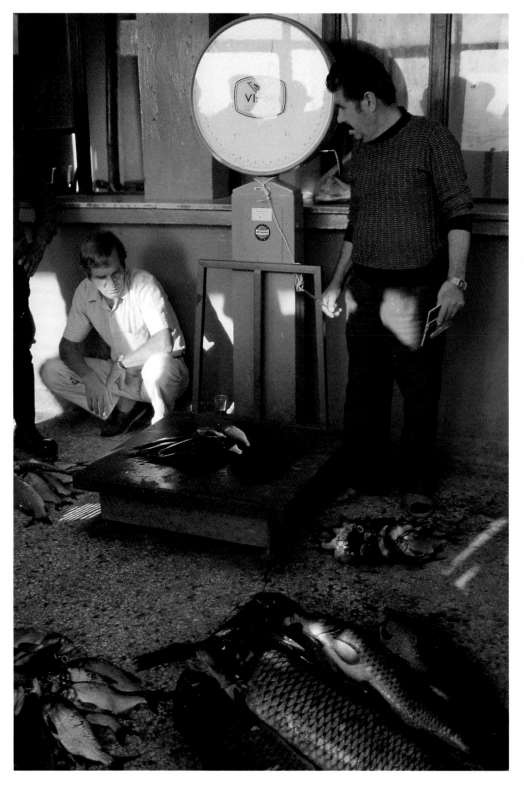

A fish market in Greece. Some of these genuine wild carp weighed over 20lb

to his younger, stronger son. A few more minutes elapsed and as the fish remained totally unstoppable, Wolfgang decided to take to a boat. The Romanian guides helped the angler into a boat and packed his companions into two smaller boats alongside. The idea was that his friends could give advice and play torch beams on to the area, for darkness was already creeping in. Also, undoubtedly, Wolfgang would need considerable help if the fish ever came to the landing stage.

The light fell but the powerful catfish continued to pull the boat out towards the Black Sea and in all the party travelled 2 miles after the fleeing giant. Soon the sea itself could be seen, glowing dimly under the night sky. The battle seemed interminable and sometimes it would take ten minutes to put 30yd of line back on to the reel – 30yd of line that could be gone again in a mere ten seconds. There was no sign of the fish tiring or coming to the surface and hours, literally, passed by. Wolfgang, although young and strong, was almost exhausted himself.

Darkness had totally fallen when the fight took on a new and dour stage. The catfish had found a deep area full of snags where it obviously felt safe. It clung to the bottom, hardly moving, as though it was collecting its strength for the final round of the fight. Wolfgang began to smoke another cigarette and the other fishermen in boats gathered round him, bringing gaffs and ropes and axes, for when such a huge cat is eventually boated it has to be killed at once or one blow from its powerful tail can virtually empty the boat of anglers.

After twenty minutes of uneasy calm, the catfish began to move, powering towards the river bank and a screen of dead trees lying in the margins. Wolfgang put on all the pressure that he could and just turned the fish. It wallowed in the shallows, showing part of its body: in the beam of the torches, it looked immense. The shallow water was working against the catfish and it could no longer keep as deep as it had done before in the open river. Each time it wallowed on the surface, it took air in through its mighty mouth and that itself made diving more difficult. Wolfgang was gaining more strength and confidence and, bit by bit, yard by yard, the catfish began to near the boat. After three-and-a-half hours of exhaustion and excitement the fish was almost at a standstill by the boat and Robert Raduta, the guide, plunged the first gaff in near the head. Immediately, Wolfgang gaffed the fish a second time down by the tail. The fish was in the boat thrashing until a blow from the flat part of the axe on the skull quietened it. Now exuberant, the boats made their way back up-river in the darkness, the fishermen laughing and joking and celebrating. A crowd gathered by the boat; beer and bottles of wine were drunk all night long. Wolfgang was so tired and yet so excited that he could not possibly sleep and, as the morning appeared, he and his friends took the enormous fish into a grocery shop in nearby Roschu. The scales stopped at a little over 212lb and, according to local custom and tradition, the fish was divided up. The head was given to Wolfgang as his trophy and the body was divided among the guides for them and their families to eat during the weeks to come.

European Carp fact file

Seasons

For much of Europe, the best carp-fishing months are from April to November inclusive. However, Lake Casein does fish very well even in December and January when the nights can be cold but the days are often pleasantly warm. Obviously, the higher altitude lakes tend to close in the winter as do those deeper in the land-mass of central Europe. Spring, summer and early autumn generally offer reliable conditions but there can be flash-floods that are capable of raising the levels of reservoirs past an easily fishable limit. For this reason, it is best to plan a trip to Europe for as long as possible. This way, arrangements can be somewhat flexible and if you are washed out on one water, you will have time to move and prospect on another.

Tackle

For the large fish in the big waters we are looking at English tackle scaled up somewhat: 12ft, 2½lb test-curve rods are generally about right but sometimes 3lb test-curve rods are called for. It is rare that lines of less than 15lb breaking strain are needed. It is not just the fish that demand heavy tackle but also the snag-ridden waters that they tend to inhabit. Obviously, only the strongest hooks should be used with such equipment and everything must be checked and rechecked so that nothing lets you down at the critical moment.

Bait

It makes sense to bait with a bed of maize. This is reasonably cheap and holds fish well. It can be taken over to Europe but is also fairly widely available locally in many areas. On top of the maize the most generally used hook-bait is, of course, a boilie. It is hard to be exact about amounts, but the general rule is to go with more than you think is necessary. Do not underestimate the capacity of these big European fish to devour enormous quantities of food.

Miscellaneous

Take care when afloat in an inflatable boat. Rain makes these very slippery and it is easy to lose balance and fall overboard. A man alone, at night, in a one-piece suit and boots can quickly be in severe trouble; always go out with a lifejacket.

Check local rules very carefully and remember that many countries and districts do not allow night fishing. Also, be careful to observe areas of wild-fowl sanctuary and make sure that you possess all the correct national licences and, if necessary, regional stamps. Sadly, in the early days of Casein, some British anglers behaved very badly and tarnished the reputation of British fishermen. Law-breaking, drunkenness, refuse and loutishness combined to make the British angler unwelcome at many places. Remember that the true carp angler appreciates everything of his surroundings, takes only photographs and leaves nothing but his footprints.

Salmon in Norway

Salmon must be the world's most famous fish and everything about their shape, size, silver sheen and life history is exotic and romantic. People who show little interest in fish profess fascination with salmon. Salmon is the fish that every tourist recognises, urging its way up the waterfalls to its spawning beds.

It is not surprising, therefore, that when many people want to fish, salmon become their ultimate target and aim. The famous rivers of the world are like Mecca to them and the thought of catching a 50lb fresh-run fish on the fly is one of the sport's greatest dreams. Today, there is only one country where this is possible: Norway. When it comes to the Atlantic salmon, Norway is unparalleled. Of course, salmon fishing today is not what it was and Norway, like everywhere else, has its problems, but those river names – the Vosso, the Alta, the Namsen and the Laerdal – still ripple with pure magic.

The early anglers in Norway were true pioneers, experiencing extreme difficulty in getting to the north of the country. British anglers began to visit there in the 1830s and the Reverend Bilton made two journeys to the Namsen, in 1837 and 1839.

In *Jone's Guide to Norway* the sort of journey an early angler could expect is described: the steamer left London for Hamburg taking sixty hours to cross the North Sea. From there, the angler travelled by carriage or rail to Kiel. After a wait a steamboat would take him to Copenhagen and from there on to Christiania, now known as Oslo. From Oslo it was steamboat to Trondheim – often with sixty-four stops en route! From there a carriage would carry the angler and his equipment at 5mph across the wildest of country. The whole journey could easily take a month, including stops – the nightlife of Hamburg even in those early days was apparently especially notable.

Fishing itself was often no easier than the travelling. Jone's describes it thus:

In order to command sport the salmon fisher must rough it. The plan is to boat up the river carrying reindeer skins, a scotch plaid and an axe – neither should the brandy flask be forgotten. Begin then by going up river about eight in the evening and fishing every pool. The fish will cease to rise about midnight. Reel up and proceed to the spot where operations are to commence in the morning. The boatmen and attendant will then light a fire and cut birch bows which they will convert into a sort of wigwam.

Norwegian salmon fishing has a long and noble sporting past. Just look at the size of these three fish, averaging over 40lb, caught in the mid-nineteenth century

Cover these over with the reindeer skins, lay down with the head to the wind and the feet to the fire. One of the boatmen must keep watch and the moment the fish begin to rise in the morning, up and at them. This is the surest method of getting sport. It is a plan we invariably adopt and we have met with great success. We do not travel so many hundred miles for nothing, neither are we idle when we arrive at our journey's end.

Mosquitoes were a particular curse and Jone's had a certain amount of practical advice to give:

These infernal enemies to repose deny any comfort and assail in myriads the unprepared stranger. We give an antidote. This is a nostrum. Beat well up in some hog's lard, oil or spirits of turpentine and carry it to the riverside in a tin canister. Having well anointed the hands and wrists, apply the mixture to face, ears and throat. Tie a silk handkerchief from the top of the head and turn it round the throat, fastening it well behind to prevent the venomous wretches wriggling down your neck. On coming into contact with the fragrant concoction the invaders will turn on their backs and give up the ghost. We anticipate the thanks of every Norwegian salmon fisher for this wrinkle.

Odd Haraldsen playing a 33lb salmon at the Rongen Pool on the Vosso

Tremendous preparations had to be undertaken for such a mammoth journey in early Victorian England and Jone's recommended two rods, one of 19ft and another of 17ft with an extra top for each rod should one be broken in transit or on a fish. Reels were expected to contain 100-120yd of line and rods were made of hickory, ash, lance wood or laminated split bamboo. Some monstrous rods could be as long as 24ft and one was measured around the butt at 5in and weighed in total 5lb!

However, the superlative quality of the fishing was enough to ensure that many English anglers made the journey to fish in the Norwegian rivers. Especially favoured was the River Alta which saw continued patronage by the Dukes of Roxburghe and Westminster and Viscount Coke and into this century by the celebrated writer Charles Ritz. I say the superlative quality of the fishing, for record book after record book (and some are still kept at Holkham Hall in Norfolk, home to this day of the Cokes), record the most extraordinary catches – 79$\frac{1}{2}$lb salmon taken on a spinner in 1928 and in 1929 Viscount Coke landed more fish over 40lb than under 20lb out of his ninety-one salmon total. Sport after World War II continued to hold up on the Alta and in 1951 Agnar Johnson landed a fish of 70lb, followed the next year by a monster of 70$\frac{1}{2}$lb. With 30-pounders average, 40-pounders common and 50- and 60-pounders merely good fish, it is hardly surprising that the Norwegian experience has continued for well over a century to be the climax of many a fly angler's life.

Of the moderns, Arthur Oglesby writes about Norway the most beautifully and most thrillingly:

> Norway in June! The magnificence of it! I'm quite lost for all the necessary superlatives: mountains, lakes and fiords; tall pines and the foaming torrents that rush, barely slowing, until they tumble into the sea.

Oglesby also relays perfectly the excitement of a Norwegian summer when the nights never really grow dark and when the temperatures are constantly 80-90°F (26-32°C). Sleep is hardly possible, both because of the conditions and the ever-present expectancy and excitement of the situation:

> I could not sleep a wink that night. Here we were on the Vosso with an odds-on chance of getting a fish that would qualify for headline status back in Britain. I felt that the Almighty had indeed been very kind to me.

But fishing in Norway is not, and never was, easy:

> The next day Nils, my gillie, arrived at 9am. It was even hotter with the mercury just short of the ninety-degree mark. Fishing in breast waders, even in shirt sleeves, is no easy task under such tropical conditions. During that morning I sweated and slaved, only to lose a good fish after playing it for a few minutes on a heavy Devon Minnow. The hookhold just gave way and I have no way of knowing if it was a monster or not. With the heat of the afternoon, fishing became impossible. I lay on my bed restlessly, waiting for the sun to lose some of its power.

All experienced fishermen know this type of situation, when hopes and optimism run high, along with very big fish, but when success has still got to be achieved. The knowledge that something important could well happen in the next session, or even on the next cast, creates an unbearable tension:

By 8pm we were back on the river, still in shirt sleeves, but with most of the shocking heat now dissipated. Nils commanded that we try the prawn. Having indulged in a certain amount of prawn fishing some years earlier, I had more or less reserved its use for poor conditions; but if it meant the possibility of getting one of those Norwegian monsters, who was I to stick to loosely held principles? On went the prawn. I was soon to learn that the sink and draw methods used on these very powerful rivers were more difficult than they had been at home; and to manipulate them correctly required some knowledge and skill. Eventually I got the hang of it again; and as Nils boated down the Upper Bolstad pool things happened. The bait stopped. As I raised the rod and felt the heavy movement I leaned over to Nils and said, 'Fish'!

This is it. This is the moment every big fish man knows when the stomach lurches and the dreams of years are about to be fulfilled:

At first I wondered if I had not, in fact, stuck on the bottom. Nothing moved. Then I felt the solid weight of a heavy fish. For ten minutes I just heaved, trying to get the fish out of the strong current. The heaving seemed to have no effect. The fish stayed where it was, apparently oblivious to the fact that it was hooked. Doubtless the prawns and hook in its mouth were little more than an annoyance. After a further ten minutes of this tug-of-war game I asked Nils to boat me down to a position where I could impose side-strain on the fish. Nils was very reluctant to do this, since it meant taking the boat dangerously near a point where he would be unable to row it back upstream again. He kept repeating, 'Verra bigg fishe – maybe twenty-three kilos?' Realising that he meant something in the region of fifty pounds, I paled at the prospect of ever getting a sight of it – let alone getting it ashore.

Eventually, however, I persuaded Nils to move down a little. The side-strain I was now able to impose on the fish began to have an effect. Slowly it moved, but used its stupendous strength to fight upstream into the really heavy water of the main current. After five minutes of this gruelling encounter it turned tail in a flash and rushed downstream. As my reel began to empty with an ever-increasing scream, Nils shouted 'It's going to the fiord.' He then rowed the boat into the main draw of the current and we set off in pursuit. The great fish continued its headlong flight downstream. As we came to the rapids, with practically all my line gone, the fish moved violently into them. Down we plunged, fish and boat together. Foaming water splashed over the gunwales of the boat as it bobbed up and down like a cork in a storm. Within a very brief period all was quiet as we smoothed out

Washing down a day's catch of salmon

on the placid waters of the fiord. Where was the fish? Winding the reel handle as fast as my hands would go, I took back the slack line and to my great delight it was still on. Now in the quieter waters, I could at least get on better terms with it, terms that would perhaps be in my favour. By this time the entire village, it seemed, was on hand to watch and offer advice. Then, at the end of a gruelling forty minutes, as the sun set behind the beautiful backdrop of mountains, Nils' gaff went home and out came my new record

Jim Deterding with a 38lb salmon from the Vosso

A remarkable, ancient photograph of two salmon weighing 103lb! Norway, amazingly, is still capable of producing such leviathans

salmon of forty-six and a half pounds. It was covered in sea lice and, to me, was the most beautiful creature in the world.

That is very special fishing, as is a day on the Alta. Fishing begins at eight in the evening and there is an air of expectancy as the boat-men arrive at the camp. Where possible, an angler who has fished the Alta before fishes with the same team of boat-men. The first night, therefore, is a time of much back-slapping and talk of last year's fish whose weight will have increased considerably over the winter months. At midnight, with the sun low over the horizon, a rest is taken, usually signalled by the boat-men calling coffee. This is a traditional picnic, very much a feature of the Alta experience. A fire, made of driftwood, is lit on the rocky shore and a brew of coffee is made in an iron kettle. Drunk from a wooden cup carved from birch wood, the taste is described as 'different'. The supper consists of a Thermos of soup, a sandwich and, most important of all, the traditional sausage. This, too, is different. After four hours in the boat it is pleasant to stretch the legs and relax. Fishing then resumes until 4am when all return to camp. The fish, which one hopes one has caught, are weighed, photographs taken, discussions and arguments settled, a few drams taken and at last bed beckons.

Norwegian fact file

The sad fact is that the great days of Norwegian salmon fishing were obviously declining from the later 1970s and in 1988 drastic measures were taken by the Norwegian government. Their own drift-nets were suspended and poaching was for the first time vigorously discouraged. The signs are – as the hopes certainly are – that these measures may well have saved Norwegian fishing, but there are still major problems experienced there. The farmers, in the main the riparian owners, have little idea of salmon as a sport-fishing pursuit. They are little schooled in ideas on river management and catch-and-release is virtually unknown to them. Most of them care little for subtlety of method and rod numbers can be high and fishing allowed on both banks. However, there is a certain amount of well-run fishing in Norway as some companies, associations and syndicates have bought up fishing on long leases and are running their waters exceptionally well.

In a nutshell, Norwegian salmon fishing is something of a mixed bag: there is no doubt that some of the country's rivers still produce the best Atlantic salmon fishing in the world but that there is a long way to go before all its rivers are better than simply moderate. But some of Norway's rivers are undoubtedly the best in the world. One particular river in one particular week in 1992 produced 190 fish averaging 26lb each for a group of anglers. This is simply outrageous fishing that equals anything from the days of Cyril Mowbray Wells.

Seasons and Times

The best seasons in Norwegian rivers depend to some extent upon altitude and how the rivers are fed, but as a generalisation the prime time tends to be from around 1 June to mid/late July.

Norway is, of course, the land of the midnight sun and in the high summer there is daylight throughout the night with often only an hour or an hour-and-a-half when the sun disappears totally. The night is obviously very much cooler and the fish tend to feed better in subdued light conditions, so for both these reasons much Norwegian fishing is done after dinner. It is dramatic, beautiful fishing and the size of the fish only intensifies the magnitude of the experience. Very often at night the river is rising as the sun has melted the snow on the mountains during the day. This can lead to problems and on some of the southern rivers, fishing in the day, especially when the sun is covered by cloud, is preferred.

Tackle

We will talk about fly fishing only here as this is what the majority of visiting sportsmen like to use. The rod should be stiff, with a fair bit of backbone to it and it is essential that the reels have a good drag system – for example, the System 2 reels or those made by Bogden. In the early part of the season, shooting heads can be useful to give both distance and depth to the fly. A fast-sinking, heavy-tube fly is not generally considered the best Norwegian type and most prefer something that retains a certain amount of life in the water – for example, a Collie.

As the season progresses intermediate lines can be used, although strictly, floating lines are probably best avoided. The flies remain large throughout the year and a floating line only tends to emphasise the problem of drag. Very big fish are taken in what can be exceptionally swift water and it is rarely advisable to drop below 25lb in leader strength.

Just as anywhere, fishing tends to be from both bank and boat and can change as the levels rise or fall.

Health

Norway is probably one of the most hygienic countries you could hope to find, but even here I am told there are problems: the beds are too narrow and the curtains

tend to be too thin! Neither seems important unless it is you yourself trying to sleep on a plank, blinded by the midnight sun.

Price

This is a key question and one that intrigues most observers. Obviously the continuing world recession is having an effect and it is difficult to be exact. They key to securing good Norwegian salmon is good references. By this, I mean that there are several bad European operators. They know that since the 1988 measures to tighten up on netting, things should be improving and they are therefore hiring mediocre water and paying huge prices for it. These prices are obviously passed on to the customer and the fishing is often moderate and disorganised and hampered by the failure of the farmers to appreciate what is desired.

Many contacts are best found through friends and word of mouth and do not advertise at all. Indeed, this is fishing the world over and not even an enormous cheque book can always buy an angler the best fishing.

There are three major ways of approaching Norwegian fishing. The first is to make enquiries and buy day-ticket fishing. Little money is involved in this and quite a few of the waters can be of very decent quality. In fact, this is a good way to make an introduction to Norwegian waters. The second way is to secure a rod on an acknowledged beat on a good week of the year. This, however, is very likely to be expensive and may cost well over £2,500. The third and all-too-frequent way of securing Norweigan fishing is to book with one of the shady operators. These characters still charge a high rate and offer fishing that is only moderate in value. The advice, therefore, is either to go for the cheap end of the market or to try to go in at the very top, if your pocket can afford it.

Of course, Norway offers more than salmon alone and is probably one of the best sea-trout countries in the world. Many of these fabulous fish grow to nearly 20lb and fishing for them is much more accessible than for their larger cousins.

Contacts

Most of the advice given in this fact file was provided by Tarquin Millington Drake who is one of the most experienced of the modern-day Atlantic salmon fishermen. In 1992 he fished for Atlantic salmon in all the countries that still boast appreciable runs.

Tarquin would be happy to advise callers on his personal telephone number 071–228 8127.

European Catfish

Like them or loathe them, the inescapable fact is that catfish do grow to enormous sizes, fight manically and are extremely interesting creatures. For myself, I like their looks even and it is one of my greatest sadnesses that I have not personally landed a big fish yet – but I will!

One man who has really taken European catfishing to heart is Derek Quirk, a Liverpudlian who really works for his fishing. The following is Derek's account of catfishing in Spain and it is a fascinating one. Above everything else, I ask you to notice the tremendous preparation that Derek and his friends put into the journey: absolutely nothing was left to chance and yet chance still played every ill-conceived trick that it could!

A deep, slow river in southern Austria – a superb catfish river

First things to sort out were two suitable fishing boats and a vehicle capable of transporting us on the 3,000-mile round trip to Spain. The relevant phone calls were made to friends in the Norfolk area and a likely sounding 10ft 'jobby' (Sheffield lingo) was soon located. Pete and Bob Lee (our photographer for Spain) elected to travel down to Norfolk to suss it out. Just as well they did, for not only did they return home with a superb 10ft fibreglass boat and a 4hp motor for less than £200, but they also managed to catch a 5lb chub EACH.

Our new boat was ideal in shape, having quite an acute bow, while at the same time sporting a fairly flat bottom. The pointed bow would certainly ease the burden of rowing upstream in such a formidable river, and the flat bottom would provide the essential stability required for playing a huge 'Siluro'. In the following weeks the boat was gradually brought up to Ebro standard, as Pete and Bob took on the joinery work such as the modification of seating, transom, gunnels etc, while I concentrated on the engineering side of things which involved making new rollocks, boat and rod rests and echo-sounder brackets.

Boat number two was to be a 10ft Avon inflatable belonging to 'John the copper' (a Sheffield policeman). Taking two boats to Spain would enable four of us to boat fish, thus leaving three people bank fishing, or, perhaps more importantly, in charge of our motor vehicle and its contents. Spanish villians are quickly cottoning on to the vast array of equipment that we English anglers tend to carry with us wherever we venture.

I was extremely sceptical of Pete and John's decision to use an inflatable dinghy, because on a previous trip Spike and I had endured the nerve-racking experience of having our boat attacked on two separate occasions by huge catfish. We put this phenomenon down to the fact that these fish are very much territorial in their behaviour and that we were probably encroaching on their territory. Certainly they couldn't have mistaken our boat for food.

Pete and John were confident that the rubber material of which the Avon was made would be strong enough to withstand anything that a Spanish 'Siluro' could throw at it. Even so, Spike and I insisted that the Sheffield lads would fish from rubber while Liverpool would be sticking firmly to the fibreglass construction.

With the boats finally sorted, the next thing on the agenda was the choice of a suitable hire vehicle. It had to be big, powerful and reliable enough to carry seven people, two boats with motors, anchors, oars etc, plus all our fishing equipment and suitcases. With economy also in mind we eventually chose a 3-litre diesel engined LWB minibus which we would pick up a day or two before the off, allowing time for us to carry out some alterations to the seating arrangements. Roger Prior (our bait-catcher for Spain) had constructed some special seats that would enable the rota of four drivers to take turns apiece at getting some sleep, hence allowing the long journey to be completed almost non-stop.

With the May deadline fast approaching we turned our attention towards tackle requirements and this was where Pete and I really seemed to gel. This was mainly due to the fact that I have the good fortune to work in an engineering machine shop and that Pete Evans is one of the most innovative anglers that I have yet to meet. Between us we soon had the ball rolling and due to my close encounter with a certain 77lb cat, giant landing-nets were our 'numero uno' concern.

Arms were made from old rod blanks that were bought and scrounged from a variety of sources, with the main criteria being that they were 6ft long, fairly light and very strong. The next job was for me to machine up some 12in wide spreader blocks out of a strong, durable plastic material called polypenco. The extra width is essential when landing a big cat, enabling its head to be drawn right up to the block to ensure that the full length of its body is totally ensconced by the net. The giant frames were complemented by a copious supply of extremely strong, wide meshed, knotless netting which was acquired by Pete (though I'd better not say where from). The wide mesh is most useful on such a large landing-net as it offers far less resistance in running water than any of the micro-mesh varieties.

Rods and reels were the next items to consider, with the latter a fairly easy choice. The superb clutch mechanisms and deep spools of the Shimano and Silstar bait-runner reels would be just the job for our Spanish cat-fishing.

To team up with the bait-runners, we needed to look no further than the superb range of telescopic rods made by Silstar. Teles are no longer the floppy monstrosities of old and I do suspect that they will soon become classed as standard equipment for fishing abroad (even for us carbon crazy English).

With a travel length of only 30in (a suitcase job) and a test curve of about 5lb, the Silstar 10ft 3304 glass tele costs just £36.99 and its powerful yet surprisingly progressive action would land any fish that swims the Ebro at the moment. With this in mind I contacted my good friend Joe Taylor, the Bicester tackle dealer, with a bulk order, and a few days later a package of sixteen telescopics duly arrived; we were in business.

As our May deadline loomed, Pete and I continued to bump up our phone bills with trans-Pennine phone calls, as we organised other important items of tackle such as special unhooking and weighing equipment.

Artery forceps would be of little use for extracting a size 5/0 hook from the jaws of a 6ft long catfish, so these were discarded in favour of long-nosed pliers with 16in extensions welded to the handles. To enable us to weigh such a monster, huge weigh-slings were cut from a tarpaulin sheet and kindly sewn up by a lady friend of mine from the sewing room where I work (amazing what a box of chocolates can accomplish). Tracking down some adequate weigh-scales certainly presented us with a problem, but a tour around the butchers' shops of Liverpool and Sheffield was eventually rewarded by a couple of sets of Salter 100kg dial scales which were bargained for less than the price of a leg of lamb.

With our tackle requirements finally complete, we then had to concentrate on the masses of paperwork relating to our trip. Ferry bookings, passports, green cards and travel insurance were all arranged in good time, and letters were drafted (in Spanish) to the appropriate authorities in the vain hope of obtaining at least one of the two boat licences required (per boat) to fish the Ebro.

The Spanish are the world's worst for red tape and along with the boat licences (one of which is an eight-page document), each angler must possess a special permit which he must sign for upon issue. For this reason they will not send them by post, meaning that on the day of our arrival we would have to travel the 80 miles from our venue to the nearest major town to obtain them. Due to the fact that the licence authority offices are closed over the weekend, it is pointless arriving in Spain on a Saturday or Sunday as the Spanish police do not take kindly to English anglers fishing without licences.

The final week prior to departure was spent with my head buried in a Spanish phrase book, as important phrases like *'siete grande cervazas por favor'* (seven large beers please) were carefully memorised. The phrase book is an absolutely essential item when visiting one of the remote inland towns of Spain, and it's rare to come across anyone who speaks a word of English.

As is often the case when travelling to such far-away places, one or two mishaps were encountered along the way, namely the combined weight of our fibreglass and inflatable boats, which were lashed to the top of the van, created so much pressure that the roof-rack began to pierce holes in the roof. This forced us to stop on numerous occasions and unbelievably we missed our 11pm Sally Line ferry crossing from Ramsgate. All we could do was wait for the early morning ferry. This had happened despite three months' planning and preparation: what a mistake to make!

However, we soldiered on and were soon enjoying a superb breakfast on the comfortable two-and-a-half hour crossing to Dunkirk. This set us up nicely for the arduous journey through France and after negotiating the notorious Paris periphery, we were subjected to the seemingly never-ending procession of signs to Lyon. Eventually we crossed the border just beyond the Pyrenees mountains, and after driving through some spectacular Spanish terrain we finally reached our destination.

We stood gazing at the mighty Rio Ebro and our fears that it may be in flood proved totally unfounded, as it flowed at a leisurely pace down from the mountains. Pete and I were confident that we could get away with using 5oz leads and that the huge supply of 8oz leads that were currently weighing down our rucksacks would not be required. The river certainly looked inviting, but unfortunately the water temperature appeared to be a little on the cold side. Hopefully, though, the present hot weather would warm up the water as the week progressed.

Our decision to include a match angler in our party proved to be a very wise one indeed, and in no time at all, Roger, whose sense of humour had

The famous River Ebro, the premier catfish river of Spain
Insert: *Derek Quirk holds a Spanish 43-pounder*

kept everyone's spirits up during the long hard journey, had caught enough small carp and rudd to keep us going in bait for the first few days. During this time, using two boats and echo-sounders, we were able to suss out the various underwater features fairly quickly, and the process was made even easier as Pete and I kept in constant contact with the aid of my walkie-talkies (a present from a young lady called Pauline).

We fished hard by day and night in the numerous likely-looking areas along a 2-mile stretch of the river below one of the many hydro-electric dams that are part of the Ebro system. The echo-sounders were invaluable for locating shallow areas close to steep drop-offs, yet despite this, the catfish seemed loath to follow their normal procedure of moving on to the shallows at night to feed.

By day four of the trip, we had turned our attentions to a back-water of the Ebro that confluences about a mile downstream of the dam, an area that is always a good bet to produce catfish. A couple more days were spent in this area, but all we could muster were a couple of dropped runs, presumably from small cats, and due to the endless problems experienced with both our outboard motors, we were all, apart from the ever-cheerful Roger, feeling very frustrated and very tired.

It's amazing how a problem can seem much worse than it actually is when you are over-tired. A good few hours' sleep were called for before we tackled the tedious task of stripping down the motors. Fellow Scouser Spike, who, like myself, is an engineer, was elected for the job and despite the limitations of our tool kit, within a few hours he somehow managed to right most of the problems.

With a sense of urgency beginning to descend upon us, we moved further up the back-water into a very narrow, shallow stretch of water where the flow became almost non-existent. Two parties of English anglers from Luton and Millwall were already fishing there and between them they had managed to catch just two fish in seven days. This was a lot better than we'd achieved, especially when you consider that their biggest fish was a 70-pounder caught by the smallest member of the Luton crew: Frank. We affectionately christened him 'French Franc', later to be changed to '50 centimes Franc' (when he took his shoes off). He may have lacked quite a few inches in height, but he lacked nothing in personality and teamed up with our own half of the comedy act: Roger. We were all certain to be amused while we awaited some action from the catfish.

The Sheffield five decided to bank-fish, as were all the Luton and Millwall lads, while Spike and I elected to fish by boat near the confluence of the narrow stretch of the backwater (complicated, isn't it?). With just three nights' fishing remaining, I loaded up the boat and set off towards a promising spot that I had sussed out earlier in the day.

Tackle consisted of Silstar 3304 telescopic boat rods and Shimano 4500 aero bait-runner reels filled with 25lb bs Berkley Big Game line. Hooks were obviously very important and I had brought a wide variety, ranging from sizes 3 to 6, with the main criteria being that they were all very strong and very sharp. For a hook-length material, I had opted for a 45lb bs Kryston Quick-silver, which under an abrasion-resistance test proved to be up to three times more abrasion-proof than any of the nylon lines I tested. It has the added advantage of being far more supple than nylon, a fact that I hoped would help to reduce the number of dropped runs often experienced when fishing for catfish. A special-purpose giant landing-net, a lifejacket and a walkie-talkie completed the set-up for a night's boat fishing.

I was soon anchored up and had cast out two baits, one a small rudd, the other a carp. Both baits were fished on straightforward rigs, one a simple running link-leger rig with a light 8lb bs lead-link just in case the lead snagged on the rocky bottom, the other a standard sunk-float paternoster arrangement as used in pike fishing.

After about half-an-hour an enormous splash at the side of the boat near caused me to jump out of my skin, and moments later another eruption further away from the boat in very shallow water did nothing to calm my nerves. I reeled in both rods and recast them accordingly before sitting back and waiting with baited breath. Fifteen minutes passed with no action so I picked up the walkie-talkie to inform Pete that we had at long last discovered an area with catfish. Immediately the bait-runner screamed and the walkie-talkie near ended up overboard as I made a dive for the rod. I had no sooner picked up the rod when the bait-runner stopped, indicating a dropped run. Pete, who had obviously heard the commotion, was desperately trying to contact me, so I reluctantly retrieved the walkie-talkie for a chat.

None of the lads bank fishing had experienced any action, but the night was still young, so we agreed to contact each other every half-an-hour to keep a check on events.

The night wore on with little activity and I decided to take the water temperature, which had been slowly creeping up during the last two days. It's Sod's Law isn't it, that the moment you do something other than stare at your rods, you get a run. This one was an absolute screamer and needless to say the thermometer ended up smashed in the bottom of the boat as I wound down into the fish. The rod lurched over and I was into what felt like a very good fish, but almost immediately the line went slack as the hook pulled out.

Things went very quiet from then on and it was comforting to be able to chat to Pete every half-an-hour or so. My watch indicated that it was 4 o'clock in the morning, but strangely I received no contact from my friend. Twenty minutes later I found out why. I'll never forget the excitement in his voice as he told me 'I've caught a siluro'. 'How big?' I asked, also with great excitement. 'I don't know, you've got the scales, but I think it's a 70,' was his reply. Little did he know how wrong he was.

At long last the months of preparation now seemed worthwhile, as Pete had obviously caught the first big fish of the trip. But how big? Pete made the decision to leave the fish in the huge wide-meshed landing-net until daylight, at which time I would motor ashore with the scales and the fish could be weighed, videoed, photographed and then released all in one go. Dawn arrived and I duly motored ashore to be met by all three of the English

A large lagoon on the borders of Austria and Germany, home of catfish to over 150lb

One of the strange phenomena of fishing in Europe: here 7 and 8in frogs attack a float

A nase – one of the staple foods of big European catfish

Lake Bled, just over the Austrian border into the old Yugoslavia; home of very big catfish

parties crowding around Peter who was anxiously waiting for the weigh-in. What an experience the next ten minutes or so turned out to be and I for one will never forget it.

As I made ready my 100kg Salter dial scales, Roger got the video into action and Pete hauled the fish out of the water with more than a little help from his long-term angling companion, big Bob Lee. Cameras galore started clicking furiously as approximately twenty anglers gazed in awe at the biggest fish that they had ever set eyes upon. Pete had without doubt underestimated the size of this fish, and I won't forget in a hurry the look on his face when I told him that his siluro was far and away bigger than the 77lb monster that I had landed for my mate Andy Flanders the previous year. Into the giant weigh-sling she went and four of us were needed to hoist her up on to the scales, which we had lashed to one of our boat oars.

By this time, the excitement and tension had reached fever-pitch and I was obviously wasting my time as I shouted at everyone to please stop swearing, as the whole event was being recorded on video. Unbelievably, the dial swung all the way round to the 100lb mark before finally settling at 98lb exactly. Much to everyone's amusement, Pete collapsed to the ground muttering the words 'What have I done?' I don't think that he was too concerned that his fish fell just 1½lb short of the Spanish record and that if he had weighed it immediately after capture it may well have beaten it.

The awkward task of taking the trophy shots was undertaken as quickly as possible before, with the aid of the giant weigh-sling, we returned the leviathan back into the river where she immediately swam away powerfully. Later that day we all took a break from the fishing and spent the afternoon in the bar celebrating Pete's fish of a lifetime.

That night our good fortune continued and all the lads were chuffed for our match angler Roger, who landed his first-ever catfish, and the fact that it only weighed 8lb did nothing to dampen his elation. I finally caught a cat myself, although at around 16lb it was hardly the fish I was after.

Lady Luck just didn't seem to be by my side on this holiday and the following morning I experienced an absolutely fascinating encounter with a larger catfish, and how I failed to catch him I'll never know. I had fished all night at the entrance to the narrow back-water and as dawn approached I decided to up-anchor and try my luck actually inside it. As I reached the spot that I intended to fish, I heard the unmistakable sound of a catfish 'training', a phenomenon that many of us had heard before in Spain, but as it occurs mainly at night-time, none of us had actually seen it happening. This very loud strange noise can be heard when a catfish feeds in shallow water and it sounds just like a steam train, hence the name 'training'.

With daylight just beginning to break, I lowered my anchor very gently because the echo-sounder indicated a depth of just 2ft of water, and for the next ten minutes sat back and watched in amazement as the catfish trained back and forth across the surface with its mouth gaping and its top jaw protruding at least 10in out of the water. The sun was now high enough in the sky, so I tackled-up a simple float rig with a rudd bait set 12in below a small slider. As I cast in, the cat (which by this time I had estimated at 50lb) continued to feed and after every scoot across and surface it returned to the same small gap in the marginal reeds, burying itself into the mud in only inches of water.

After what seemed like an age it finally hit my bait and the water erupted, leaving a massive cloud of bubbles and silt as my estimation of 50lb quickly grew to 60. I couldn't believe my eyes when the split second I was about to strike, the float bobbed back up and 'el Siluro' went scurrying back to his little hole in the reeds.

It was a good two hours before he dared venture from his retreat again and by this time it was a scorching hot day. What happened next I still find hard to believe. After making another unsuccessful attempt at devouring my bait, he bolted straight under the boat (in 2ft of water) and came out the other side before circling round and heading back to his lair. I let the silt, clouds of bubbles and my heart-beat settle before, in desperation, casting in as close as possible to his favourite hide-out. The bait must have hit him smack on top of his head and he tore off along the river, causing a massive water displacement (70lb if he was an ounce). Needless to say, my siluro never returned, but I certainly will – next year!

The Huchen

The huchen is a magnificent animal. I have only ever been fortunate enough to see one and that was certainly not on the end of my line. I was fishing a tributary of the Danube one wet day in August when, far out, in the run from a massive weir, leapt a huge silvery fish. It leapt twice more and I was at a loss to identify it. I had made friends with an Austrian angler and he told me that the fish was a huchen, one of a now very rare breed.

The huchen has also been called the Danubian salmon for the species is restricted entirely to that river and its major tributaries. Attempts to introduce them to the Rhine, Elbe and Thames have all failed – although one or two fish were hooked in the Thames some years after the original stocking. The huchen is salmon-like in appearance, although its body is probably narrower and its head often larger. It grows to the same sort of

Huchen fishing is a sport of the coldest weather when the ice crackles and snow is in the air. This 40lb fish was taken in the deepest winter

enormous sizes and 30–50lb fish are possible, even in today's pressurised times.

Their range seems to be mainly confined to the middle and upper reaches of the Danube and the faster areas of the major tributary rivers. The fish spawn on gravel beds in the fastest flowing, streamy areas during the spring. The young live in small feeder streams, feeding on insects until, after a short time, they are large enough to move out into the main river and begin to feed on fish. An angler who manages to catch a huchen these days is fortunate for they are extremely sensitive to pollution and oxygen deficiency, so during recent years they have begun to disappear rapidly from places where they were once abundant.

The adult huchen is almost totally fish-eating and probably preys heavily upon the nase which frequent huchen-favoured areas in large shoals. Like the nase, the huchen likes fast water and looks for deep, snag-ridden areas in which to hide before coming out to roam and ambush its prey.

To any European angler, the huchen is a prize beyond words and my great friend Rainer Bouterwek has caught his fair share. However, to get the huchen message across to us in its full drama he describes an event that will live with him all the days of his life.

Rainer's story begins on the River Muna near the weir at Fandau. This is situated on a 20-mile stretch of Association water and became notorious as the home of a remarkable huchen. The fish had been hooked by several anglers and had been seen often enough for an estimate of 70–80lb to have been made. This was the 'giant in shining copper', as Rainer called it, that he set out so determinedly to catch.

A handful of weather-beaten huchen fishermen had been trying very hard for this trophy, for the notorious Muna huchen, in the German winters. A few of these men even succeeded in hooking the fish but every encounter ended in the huchen's victory as the unhappy anglers were either broken or their strongest trebles were straightened. The last angler to have fallen victim to the power of the fish was a new friend of mine, George, who had fallen into the river in December when trying to get to terms with the fish in an evil snag. Now, the exact lie of the huchen – as all huchen lies are – was kept top secret by each and every angler, but George hinted that the big fish would probably live in a deep channel in mid-river, protected in some way opposite the pile of rubble known as the Mona Spitz. I found the place I felt that he meant but every attempt to get a heavily leaded bait down there inevitably led to lost tackle. Mine were just some of the thousands of plugs, spinners and fish baits left useless in the river.

I began to investigate trying from the opposite bank, in Bavaria. George suggested that this line of attack would be better when the river was low, for, as he said, nobody tried from that side. It would involve a very long walk and did not even look like a huchen lie.

My mind was made up to go for the seemingly invincible huchen in winter and to travel as often as possible for it. Seasons passed without a huchen being interested in my baits and time after time I was off to try again.

A typical winter huchen lie

A huchen – the splash of silver to the right – comes to the net

At last the day dawned. It was a promising day for huchen fishing, presenting ideal conditions – a long period of severe frost was over and wet snow was flurrying down from deep hanging clouds. I was in good company, as so often, with my late friend Tony. He was not a fisherman but a helping hand and an expert at that. I bought some fresh chub from my tackle shop and these I was going to use dead on a spinning and wobbling trace. Our plan was to try a well-known huchen spot and move on to two or three more dangerous areas on the deep outer side of river bends. All of them were huchen lies on the wild, upper area of my Association water.

When we arrived with our snow chains on we found we were following a pair of fresh tyre prints in the snow and we came across a huchen angler tackling up. In front of us the river ran down to its bare bones. The ice that had formed on its edges was hanging over, cracking and piling up in places.

The reduced flow would only last through the morning, the angler told us, because of work up-river. The river was being held back at the sluices and in the afternoon the water would be flowing again normally and the levels would again rise.

'The Muna huchen – the Bavarian bank,' Tony whispered. Immediately I was struck by the same idea. We sped off to the Bavarian bank.

The walk in waders in deep snow through the wood was a long and exhausting one. We had to hurry before the water returned to normal and that only increased the pressure on us. When we got there it didn't look like a pool with a huchen hide at all. The flow was swift and everywhere there was the cracked ice on the margins. It was only when we walked cautiously into the river that we realised we were on a blade of flint which extended out fifteen metres up and down the river and reached almost to the middle. In effect we were on a roof of rock.

The water came to the top of our thigh boots and carefully moving along this ledge of rock we came to its edge from where we could see the bottom of gravel and stones eight feet down in the middle of the river. There was no doubt that we were tiptoeing on the roof of a gigantic rock cave – most certainly the stronghold of the Muna huchen.

We both knew that the great fish's lair was literally beneath our feet and we kept very, very quiet. We felt sure that even if the great fish wasn't living there another huchen or two would be. Such an ideal lie would be undisturbed and impregnable in the normal flow of the river. Though there were only a handful of huchen in the Association water a special hide like this would be a certainty for at least one fish.

This was the suspected residence of the Muna huchen itself, but was it at home now, and would it take a bait, as huchen generally only take freely when they ambush fish outside their hides? Had the disturbance on its roof been noticed? Was it alarmed by such low water? Would it be interested in food anyway? All these questions would find their answers in the next few minutes and I remember the tension.

The problem of fishing under the roof was clear as daylight. I would have to cast upstream and let the current sweep the bait back into the cave. The line would glide back to me along the ledge of the rock roof. Proper control of the bait would be impossible until it passed downstream under my feet and virtually beneath me. Whispering and tiptoeing I chose the largest chub and hooked it with two large sharpened trebles to a wire trace. The chub was about twelve ounces and was mounted through the gill cover and the back fin. Two heavy leads were pushed into its mouth and I sewed it up carefully.

The tension was unbearable when I cast the bait twenty metres upstream to be swept by the river into the cave beneath our feet. The line glided back along the ledge of the rock roof and everything went as I had hoped for. However, I lost control of the bait as it passed into the cave and I could no longer keep any type of contact. I reeled up some line to regain tension and I realised that I was snagged. My rod bent and Tony asked me what was the matter. I told him I was snagged and I tugged totally in vain, wondering how the devil I would get unsnagged without alarming the fish – if it were there beneath us in the cave. I tugged again, this time gently. No use. I jerked angrily. No result. I jerked violently five times. A result. I experienced a wild counter jerk which tore the rod down around the rock ledge into the water. This was not a snag, it was the Muna huchen. I struck as hard as possible but contacted nothing and I nearly stumbled in the swift water and lost my balance. The only affect of the strike was to pull the bait clear of the cave into the water in front of my boots, six feet below. It was followed instantly by a gigantic huchen. It was an absolutely enormous fish in shining copper armour. The huchen dashed for the bait with blown-up gill covers and seized it and shook it violently. It tore the bait into pieces which began to trundle out of sight, down-river.

The whole uproar lasted only a few seconds but Tony and I stood for a minute after the Muna huchen had turned and glided back into the cave in total silence. All Tony could say was, 'There was the Muna huchen.'

Why didn't those hooks catch hold? The answer was that the bottom treble hook had pulled out and slipped to the head of the bait when the huchen had made its wild counter-jerk. This wily fish had not grown large for nothing: it had seized the bait where there had been no hooks.

The Muna huchen had not taken that chub out of hunger for otherwise it would have gulped it in an instant. Rather the fish was enraged that such small fry had entered its territory. It had reacted like a dog defending its hut. The Muna huchen had attacked to destroy not to eat.

Tony suggested that we wait half-an-hour and then try again. I mounted a new chub but often though I let this drift down through the rock cave again, in the following two hours the fish gave no further indication. Rapidly rising water brought further attempts to an abrupt end in the early afternoon and we had to flee from the rock roof to seek protection. The castle of the Muna huchen had become impregnable again.

Regretfully, I never saw the river low enough for another try. Nobody ever caught the Muna huchen. Some anglers, very experienced ones, hooked it occasionally again in the future but it gave them all a remarkable lesson. The Muna huchen almost certainly died a natural death.

Huchen fact file

Tackle

Tackle appears to be a simple item: strong spinning gear is all that is needed, so a decent pike or carp rod, good-sized reel and variety of plugs and lures should be all that is necessary. The key to successful huchen fishing is more sophisticated than any concentration on gear.

Season

The crux of understanding huchen fishing is the weather: the huchen are only catchable after the autumn leaves have fallen and the first frosts have set in. There are simply too many food fish available to them in the summer to make them take any chances with anything that acts unnaturally.

Central European winters are frequently very cold and as a result the huchen rarely show themselves at this time. This is where the most detailed knowledge of the river is absolutely essential. The huchen have very well-defined hides and lies and they simply leave these periodically to roam the river and maintain their body fuel. The key to huchen fishing is finding these lies and putting a bait close by. Without a knowledge of the lies, huchen fishing becomes a miserable hit-and-miss affair for a species that is now very rare.

It is this winter-feeding characteristic that makes huchen fishing a near impossibility for the visitor: most associations, in Germany anyway, allow visitors tickets until around 1 October but thereafter close the waters for the benefit of their members alone. The angler visiting in the winter, therefore finds most possible waters closed to him. Before travelling to the Danube or its tributaries it is therefore essential to ensure that fishing will be available.

Spinning for huchen on a cold day

PART II:
Asian Journeys

Mahseer –
the Beginnings

British officers, civil servants and professionals who worked in nineteenth-century India were often sorry people. Oppressed by heat and filth, menaced by disease and an alien population, deprived of their childhood comforts, they naturally felt frequent needs for escape, for the chance to wring some pleasure out of this difficult existence.

Summer temperatures at low altitudes were particularly hard to bear and an annual migration to the northern hills took place. Kashmir was the favourite playground of all, where Europeans could enjoy a rich social life in the gardens, on the riverside promenades and at the polo ground of the ancient capital Srinigar. Some of the more adventurous ventured deeper into the Himalayas, shooting, trekking and fishing – often for brown trout, introduced from Scotland at the turn of the century to make up for a generally uninteresting stock of local fish. There was, however, one species that proved an important, exciting exception. In the high rivers, especially in the upper Ganges and its tributaries, swam a great Indian fish, a worthy successor to the salmon of home, for which, we know, their hearts so often ached.

This 'Asian salmon' was the golden mahseer, a massive fish. It was carp-like and fully covered with huge brassy scales that were torpedo shaped to forge the storming snow-melt rivers that thundered from the Himalayas. Raj sportsmen began to realise the potential of a fish that could measure up to 7ft long and weigh a possible 100lb and capable of a fight more heart-stopping, more back-breaking than any other freshwater fish in the world.

By the 1890s the mahseer had established itself with the tiger as one of the two major sporting prizes of the sub-continent. Soon the fish achieved a salmon-like cult status. Writers eulogised: the mahseer's first rush was that of a run-away bull. The renowned Northumbrian firm of Hardy's shipped out specially made rods and reels to deal with the Asian monster. Highland Tay, Dee and Don found their counterpart in the Himalayan Kosi, Beas and Jumna, but the Asian Spey of them all was the Ganges itself.

Victorian fishermen flocked to the Ganges during September as the monsoons began to fail. They discovered that the mahseer swim the rain-swollen tributaries to their spawning beds in mid-summer. As the rains peter away, the tributaries fall and the fish drop back to the parent river. These anglers ambushed the big fish at confluences where they rested before travelling hundreds of miles towards the Bay of Bengal.

(page 79) *Much of the best Nepali mahseer water can only be reached by raft*

A typical camp scene of nearly one hundred years ago, taken in the Himalayas

A very rare photograph, from the 1920s, of the world record mahseer of over 120lbs

The author plays a big Ganges mahseer in the shadow of the Black Rock

One particular junction became famous – the majestic Black Rock confluence. Here, at a tributary mouth, in mid-Ganges, reared a towering stone 10ft above the water surface. In the shadow of that rock the greatest of the Ganges mahseer were hooked and even occasionally landed.

Old books given to me as a child described the place and the fish with awe, and a vision of the jungle, the shrines, the great green river and the mighty mahseer flooded my young consciousness. Mahseer were the stuff of my dreams, fish whose scales were used as playing cards, whose mouths could engulf an uncut grapefruit and whose muscular bodies and tireless fins propelled them through a life of countless thousands of water miles.

Indian independence in 1947 saw the virtual end of this sporting tradition. The mahseer rivers were dammed, polluted, netted and dynamited. Hillside deforestation resulted in a wickedly quick rain run-off and the force of water flushed away the gravel used by the fish as spawning beds. By the 1960s the mahseer was a disappearing species in much of India and only a few Anglo-Indians continued to fish for them. Yet the rumour was that mahseer still lived by the Black Rock. In 1979, a young Englishman, Paul Boote, made a nine-month journey to discover whether there was truth in the tales. Ten years later, he and I were commissioned to make a film, following the Raj footsteps to the Black Rock.

By early September 1989, we had been in India nearly three weeks and were sitting in a hotel in Dehra Dun, an old hill station on the fringe of the Himalayas. It was still raining with relentless force. We had only two remaining weeks of budgeted time and the Ganges was still in full flood. That was when we realised what an audacious project we had embarked upon. Not only were we at the mercy of the weather but we couldn't guarantee that those Black Rock mahseer still existed. However, with the very first rays of the sun we left the drenched, sodden-track town, away to the near-forgotten destination in the hills.

It was the next day, as we began the trek to the river, that my dream from childhood began to unfold. Here in the sweating rainforest I had become a Raj adventurer, walking as one of the troop of porters and mountain ponies towards a village without roads, electricity, sanitation or the sight of a European for a decade.

At the valley floor, by the tributary mouth, there was no Black Rock – the hideously swollen Ganges had seen to that! Then, far out, all tousled with white plumes of rushing water, we made out the very tip of the stone's head. Now we had days of waiting before the waters would drop and the mahseer would run.

Paul Boote returns a mahseer to the green waters of the Ganges

It was no wonder that the Anglo-Indians escaped the heat of the plains for scenes such as this

The tension showed in us all and it was a time for forced patience, for playing football with the village children by the river on the ever-growing sand beach; for visiting the clay-walled village and taking tea with the elders, and for walking the jungle paths to the temples, jealously guarded by the goat-bearded wise men. Our appearance had triggered a carnival atmosphere. The camp was constantly surrounded by children as their tiny school had all but closed. The village shop-keeper did not sell an object for ten days but followed me like a puppy from dawn to dusk, often stroking my back through sheer affection and taking my hand to guide me past any possible danger on the mountain trails. Dry weather was critical, but each afternoon the searing heat piled clouds around the peaks and by darkness storms would crackle up the valleys. Perhaps a sprinkling of heavy raindrops would fall, but, night after night, the starlit skies would clear and the next dawn would come in cold but dry. Seam by seam the Black Rock revealed itself. When its haunches were visible, Paul told us to expect action and villagers confirmed that they had seen big fish leaping close to the junction. The whole camp was quiet that evening and sleep for most of us was impossible. Was the mahseer going to live up to its reputation? Would our tackle and our skill be enough to tame this fish of legend?

Two very large mahseer caught during the period just before World War I

Daybreak was pewter and still, like all the others, but the Ganges was now clearer, slower and down to the Black Rock's thighs. We began to fish like the sportsmen of old, casting a plug well out into the river and letting the current work it downstream with the enticing flutter of small prey in distress.

Deep down in mid Ganges that morning my plug was seized by a fish that exploded all my childhood fantasy and threw the fragile pieces high into the bright Himalayan light. The reality of hooking the mahseer was pain: pain on the fingertips as they searched to slow the screaming reel; pain on cut legs as they scampered over the stones of the shore in pursuit of the fleeing giant; pain of the shoulder as the rod arm heaved to hold the fish from the rapids; pain in the back as the whole body strained to lift the fish from the sanctuary of the boulder-strewn river-bed. Pain bitter-sweet as the Indian gillies lifted the fish from the waters, as the sun played on its armour-plated flanks, brushing crimsons, peaches and golds into one fabulous, unforgettable image. For three days we caught and we lost fish in the shadow of the Black Rock. A film had been made and dreams had been fulfilled. The ghosts of my angling past had been laid and, most important, we had proved the continuing existence of the Himalayan golden mahseer.

One of the scenes that triggered Richard's obsession to fish the Ganges – the author and Paul Boote admire one of the mahseer caught in the filming of 'Casting for Gold'

About Mahseer

Whereas the mahseer of the Himalayan rivers tend to be long and lean, those in the south are much deeper and heavier and carp-like. Their very size makes them impressive and their weight can make them virtually unstoppable when they reach the fast water at the tails of the slower pools.

The term 'the mighty Mahseer' first appeared in 1903 in a book on Indian angling written by an Englishman who used the pen-name Skene Dhu. However, for at least a century before this book, the most magnificent of India's freshwater gamefishes had captured the imagination of British sportsmen. The mahseer was a true Indian salmon and in 1873 Henry Sullivan Thomas actually compared the two species and said that pound for pound the mahseer was superior in sporting qualities to the salmon of his native land.

Book after book was written on mahseer while the Raj existed and Hardy's began to export special rods, reels, lines and hooks for the task of landing such big fish in rapid water.

This was the golden age of mahseer fishing, especially in the south. The state of Karnataka alone has produced over a dozen mahseer of over 100lb in weight. Also, since 1904, all the largest mahseer taken on rod and line have come from either the Cauvery or the Kabini rivers in that state. Indeed, whereas 50lb is very big for the Himalayan fish, there are times when even 100lb seems common in the south! Certainly, the list of big fish is overwhelming.

In 1870, G. P. Sanderson, the author of *Thirty Years Amongst The Wild Beasts of India*, caught a mahseer on the River Kabini on a handline which he estimated at 150lb. The head and skin of the fish were presented to the Bangalore museum, where apparently they can still be seen. Perhaps 150lb was an exaggeration, but certainly the fish weighed around 110–120lb. In 1906, however, the first 100-pounder on rod and line was caught by C. E. Murray Aynsley and weighed 104lb. A commemorative stone marker was erected on the banks of the river at the spot where the fish was landed. The same gentleman also had the luck or skill to land a 103-pounder in September 1909. He took this second fish spinning – probably one of the only 100-pounders not to come out on the traditional ragi paste.

Ten years later the most talked about and written about fish in Indian angling history was caught. This was a 119lb mahseer taken from the Cauvery in December 1919 by Major J. S. Rivett-Carnac. Rivett-Carnac was not an experienced angler and on the day in question he was broken four times by fish until a fellow angler gave him a heavier line. A little before breakfast Rivett-Carnac hooked his big fish and the battle was hectic but short-lived. On its first rush, the mahseer went 125yd down-stream and Rivett-Carnac did not move a yard after it; rather, he dug in and he heaved. The fish heaved back and the struggle, as can be imagined, was frantic. It was, however, soon over, this time in the fisherman's favour.

Probably the greatest mahseer fishermen of the early twentieth century were the Van Ingens. Father and son both caught huge fish and their results as a team make awe-inspiring reading: 107lb in January 1920; 104lb and 81lb on 4 January 1923; 100lb and 102lb in January and February 1927; 92lb and 71lb in February 1933; 96lb in 1933, and 120lb in 1946.

Other 100-pound-plus fish fell to P. V. Bowering, the Deputy Commissioner of Mysore in 1919 and to Lieut-Col G. Hare in 1926. Sir Stewart Pears went to the Cauvery on 21 January 1927 and landed a 108lb mahseer, while in 1938 Mr A. E. Lobb landed a fish of 110lb from the Kabini.

What incredible fish these must have been, but after Indian independence everything went quiet on the mahseer front. Sport fishing seemed to be a thing of the past and mahseer began to suffer greatly in new India from pollution, from damming of headwaters, from netting and dynamiting and from soil erosion from the hillsides that eventually choked the feeder and the spawning beds that the mahseer had used for generations. Indeed, it began to seem that the fabulous days of 'the mighty Mahseer' were a thing of the past.

In the 1970s things began to change. Rumours began to circulate that mahseer were still to be caught from the south, and in the middle of that decade Paul Boote made an epic journey to India. He spent nine months in the country travelling by a cart and local bus, often sick, often desperately poor. Frequently his faith flagged but he never gave up and, at last, he located mahseer. He wrote of his journeys in *Angling* magazine and the series fired a whole generation of fishermen with wanderlust. Jeremy Wade was one of those in at the beginning of the mahseer revival along with Paul and in 1986 landed a 95-pounder from the south. In 1988 a 94-pounder fell to Anthony Isaaks, and John Watson from Kent landed an 88lb mahseer in 1989.

It was in 1988 that John Wilson and Andy Davison began to fish the Cauvery intensely and between them they have caught two 90-pounders, two 80-pounders and many others over 40lb. Fishing like this just cannot long be ignored. My own first trip to the Cauvery took place in 1991 and the very first fish that I hooked from there broke my rod just above the butt before breaking the line just above the hook. In all, I was attached to the fish for some fifteen minutes, ten minutes of which I was actually swimming after it down-river. This was a particular skill that I was later going to perfect. A week later I hooked another large mahseer in exactly the same

Away from the hot dry plains, northern India can seem more water than land
The upper reaches of a mahseer river – shallow, fast and cold, rushing straight from the mountains

place and this time, knowing that I could not hold it, decided to follow it. My guide that day was one of the best known of the modern Indian mahseer maestros – Subhan. Never have I been more thankful for a talented fishing companion. That mahseer simply ran me ragged. After 10yd of white water it attached itself firmly to a sunken tree and all seemed lost. Not a bit of it! Subhan dived like the sleek water otter he is, found the line to the fish, broke it and retied it to the line direct from the rod tip. The battle started once more! We followed the fish for some 80–100yds over crevices, down water shoots, into little slacks and then away again in a pell-mell of spray and panic. The fish became snagged a second time, this time around a great boulder. Again Subhan did his diving trick and again we were off, down-river towards the final big pool.

Here at last the three of us – me, Subhan and the mahseer – floundered. All of us, I guess, were exhausted. I remember sitting on a rock, the rod barely bent at all, my head spinning, my whole body bruised and battered. Subhan kept me going: 'Pump, Sir. Keep pumping.' I did. The rod took on the curve yet again and way out in the middle of this crystal-clear pool a massive shape of golden scales rose to meet the Indian sun. This was my gigantic mahseer. The last ten minutes of that battle I will always treasure as the great fish came ever closer and grew ever clearer. Finally, it simply wallowed in the crystal water by my feet, the spinner hanging in its mouth and gleaming in the sun.

Joy plays a large mahseer as the sun begins to set

The beaten fish is held for a moment

Steve Harper grimaces as he bears the weight of his 104lb fish

In India or Africa you will find your guide is ever-present, ever-cheerful and ever-helpful

Subhan waded out and lifted the fish clear of the water and slid it on to the sand. I lay beside it quite shattered by the experience and then whooped with joy and danced in the sun–baked valley.

Foolishly, we had come without scales or even a stringer and all we could do was to estimate the size of the fish: 60lb, or perhaps 70lb, said Subhan. That was enough for me. At that point the weight of the fish was purely incidental and absolutely irrelevant. All that mattered to me was that I had caught a huge mahseer.

The remaining days of that fabulous journey passed in a whirl. Soon my fishing partner Joy was catching mahseer – two 40-pounders and a superb silver 30-pounder. Some of the fish looked bigger than the woman herself and how she ever managed to land them, I was never quite sure. Perhaps it was all down to the magic of that place, deep in the Indian jungle, and, of course, the help and advice of those marvellous Indian gillies.

What we did not know in that glorious time, was that our little party would soon create mahseer history. Johnny Jensen joined us from Denmark and he, too, soon began to catch mahseer. One dawn he decided to try the river downstream and with Subhan, cycled off down the dusty track to the nearest village 12 miles away. Little more was thought about him during the day as yet another near 50-pounder came to our rods, but towards evening his journey came straight back into focus. He rolled like a Dervish into the camp shouting and yelling and waving his arms. He would not talk until he had had a beer, for the ride through the dust and the heat had parched his throat like a desert. Finally, after minutes of suspense, he was able to talk. 92lb! Almost 4½ft long! A fight that lasted over 2½ hours in one of the smallest, most rapid pools on the entire river. At times he had been so exhausted that Subhan had taken the rod and then the Indian himself had been in danger of losing his foothold and being dragged into the river by the great fish. Over and over it seemed as if the mahseer would make just those few yards to a waterfall; once over that the battle would have been at a juddering end. But between them, Dane and Indian, they had held on to the end and landed a truly monstrous fish.

Our stay would surely offer nothing more, but then, one morning, Steve Harper decided to meet the sunrise at Crocodile Pool. We decided not to join him but fished the great pool outside the tents themselves – we made a mistake by staying so close to home. News travels fast in the jungle. Goatherders passing by whispered of a big fish caught down-river. A wise man walking to a shrine held his arms wide apart and pointed down the Cauvery. Some children ran past yelling and shouting of a big fish. We could stand it no longer and set off down-river.

We found Steve, his partner Dave Plummer and their guide Bola, all in a state of exhaustion and shock. Something huge was tethered to their rope by their feet. Steve told us the story. His reel began to scream like never before and the line rapidly emptied from the spool. There was hardly any line left and Bola ushered him to the coracle as they chased the fleeing giant, now 150yd distant. An unseen irresistable power pulled the coracle slowly into mid stream and Steve found it impossible to exert any real pressure. They were simply being towed by the fish. They were drifted and dragged downstream, gradually gaining on the fish and putting more valuable line on the spool.

Now the fish began to turn towards the left-hand bank, moving more slowly and frequently sounding in the very deep, slow-moving channel. Bola beached the coracle and got Steve on to dry land where more pressure could be exerted. Steve was now feeling more in control, but the fight was far from over. He crouched over and over, the rod pushed into his groin and then he would straighten and pump for all his worth. The pain grew intense and the heat scorched his back. After half-an-hour they at last gained their first glimpse of the fish in a gigantic flash of criss-crossed gold deep down beneath the surface. It was only a momentary sighting for it was gone again and more hard-won line was lost in the din of the screeching reel. That first sighting utterly staggered both men. It was more whale than fish and they knew that they were close to landing the fish of a lifetime: an historic mahseer.

'How big?' We peered down the rope into the depths as Bola slowly pulled it in foot by foot. Not one of us was prepared for what we saw that morning as the kites wheeled overhead in the deep blue sky. Steve had caught a mahseer of 104lb! This was a fish from the days of the Raj, the sort of mahseer that none of us ever expected to witness again. Words here are

Johnny Jensen with hat and 90lb mahseer

pointless. This is one of those cases when a photograph is worth a thousand words and not even a photograph can convey the electricity and excitement of that historic moment.

Of course, a trip to India is about more than fish – even Goliaths like this. The skies are filled with the most magical birds and the monkeys steal fruit from the tables in the camps. In the silky black night, the panthers roar and the herds of elephant trundle past the tents, so close that you can hear the dung drop and smell the dust rise from their huge feet. Life is marvellous with friends, European and Asian, eating and laughing, drinking and sleeping, and above all wandering and fishing. Bathe in the milk-warm river, or drift downstream in a coracle watching for a crocodile dozing on the big rocks. Climb the hills to watch the sun set magnificently over the valley and then go back to dream of the shrieking reel and the bucking rod totally out of your control.

The Mahseer of Nepal

Never-ending peace and love: such was the epithet given to this delightful Himalayan kingdom by the hippies who flocked into Nepal a few years after it was opened up to foreigners in the 1950s. Marijuana, romantic nights along Kathmandu's Freak Street and cheap living attracted many of the adventurous teenagers of the late Sixties – some of my own friends included. Along with the long-haired and unwashed came the climbers and the trekkers, for Nepal is literally the 'roof of the world'. Everest, Annapurna, the other 8,000m mountains, the glaciers, the rhododendron-drenched valleys and the long, sun-kissed ridges naturally proved irresistible once the country became accessible.

The hippies still exist in their faded way in the squares of Kathmandu and the mountain-men fly into the city's small airport in droves, and after my recent visit I predict that the high Himalayas will be seen as the centre of mahseer fishing. As I discovered, however, often extremely painfully, nothing so demanding comes easily, but the challenge and potential of Nepali fishing is enormous. There is certainly enough pleasure among the pain to draw me back repeatedly to those high Asian rivers.

The flight to Kathmandu is not especially comfortable, particularly if, like me, you take a cheap flight – for example, ten hours in Moscow airport at night can be a grim experience. The lights are turned energy-saving low and a three-hour wait in a gloomy restaurant is rewarded by a slice of luncheon meat, one of cucumber and one of dry bread, none of which really

Himalayan city

nourishes at three in the morning. Thank goodness for that Irish bar that stays open half the night and serves Guinness and toasted sandwiches under a sign proclaiming Cork to be 1,220 miles to the west. At the time it is enough to make you sob for Corrib.

Kathmandu is, of course, as crazy, colourful, mangy, stimulating, noisy, pell-mell, beautiful, pitiful and unforgettable as any other Asian city. This is a city of temples by the yard, one of which gave sanctuary to a young man swinging a hundred-pound block of granite on his private parts until my eyes watered for him. The streets are hives of auto rickshaws and the capital is one of clamouring traders. Pariah dogs lie in the dust and beggars raise their leprous stumps for a rain of rupees and you are always glad to leave by plane for the remote airstrips on the fringes of the country.

On my first visit it was the windy season in Nepal and the tiny twin-engined Otter had to rise massively high to clear the jagged mountain ranges. Turbulence tossed us around like a bird in a storm, the engines droned on and one by one we reached for the bags in front of us. Even the co-pilot was sick, slumped over his controls, which was good for our confidence!

After a kangaroo landing, we were bundled into a waiting jeep, white, shaken and weak. On that unforgettable first trip to Nepal, four hours of nightmare over roads cavernous enough to swallow a crocodile, we reached at last the headwaters of the river. It was night, cool, and the crickets called to a rising moon. Our tent was up, our food was cooking and along the water's edge, fish were flipping. Our reconnaissance to Nepal was finally on.

Our plan was confirmed over the campfire that night with our three excellent Nepali guides, Mangal, Pasang and Jerry. We were to raft over 100 miles down one of the highest, remotest rivers in Nepal to the confluence with the mighty Karnali, the principal tributary of the Ganges and the second largest river in Nepal. We were to fish and prospect as we went, camping on beaches at night and seeing countryside that very few Europeans had ever witnessed. Mahseer were our prime quarry, but catfish and what other surprises might come our way would be cherished. Of surprises, there were several. We were told by the men that the early rafting was hazardous and at some of the rapids there was a one-in-three chance of capsizing. Even this fear, though, was not strong enough to ward off sleep as we lay stretched out and shell-shocked beneath the stars. I woke at first light and saw the river properly for the first time. It was vicious and full-blooded, rather like a Yorkshire Dales river in a high raging winter flood. The river was, in fact, rising. We had arrived at the hottest part of the year, when the blazing sun was melting snow in the high Himalayas and this brought down gaspingly cold water, which, in the event, did little to improve our fishing, as we found later.

Next morning our belongings and ourselves were strapped to the raft and

A typical Himalayan river, here flowing a little milky from a glacier melt

A more gentle view of the river bank as breakfast is prepared
The author plays a big mahseer from a raft

The sun rises on a beautiful mahseer river

it was the second rapids that caused all the commotion. The guides beached us and walked off to plan a course through the hundred yards of wild, white water. I took the opportunity to fish the tail of the run as it swept smoothly towards the rocks, always prime mahseer water. On the fourth cast I was into a big fish that just would not be coaxed up-river. Nor could it be allowed down-stream in the fashion of fishing the waters of southern India. To try to follow a big fish through such rapids would be to break every bone in a man's body. I had to hold on and a tail came clear of the water. It was a mahseer and a big one, too big with the force of that water behind him. I reeled-in a fluttering line as the guides came back, grimly confident. We pushed off into what was literally the unknown. For a full minute my senses were all a-whirl and then I was aware of the front of the raft rearing up vertically, lost in a wall of white water. It teetered as though to fall backwards, but then made the ridge and crashed down into the trough of water behind. 'God, that was something.' I turned round to Joy, my constant Indian travelling partner. Joy? There was no Joy and no Mangal either; nor was there half the luggage.

Thankfully, the raft's load was gathered in piece by piece at the end of the run: Joy, wet, speechless and shaken; Mangal, pale beneath his brown; an oar, a half-drowned hat and a slowly revolving flip-flop. We dried out under the baking sun, simply happy to be alive, reunited and still raring to go.

Over the days the pace became less exacting as the valley widened, the gradients levelled off and the river grew to the width of the Thames in London. Small villages began to appear, scattered amid jungle and hill; tiny children cried in terror as our raft approached, fleeing from the white-skinned aliens, who were no doubt descended from the moon or the stars. We saw mahseer, big ones, rolling in shallower, faster water and hunting small fish at the margins at dusk, but such had to be the pace of our progress that fishing was snatched and much of the best water was rafted across without proper investigation. I bumped the second big fish to come my way and had odd small ones as on and on we paddled, using the sinuous current to cover mile upon mile of water each day.

At last, one late, golden afternoon, our river joined with the great River Karnali where it wound massively across the vast Terrai plains. The scale of the environment was beyond my experience. The river was like the Rhine and the plain itself appeared to last forever, stretching into the distance on every side until it was lost in the heat haze that shimmered from just after dawn and blotted out the distant mountain ranges completely. The banks were of sand and gravel and the lapwings and Nepali terns made this inland river seem more like an estuary. Villages were perched on the edge of the forest surrounded by fields of rice and maze and dotted with banana trees, cattle, goats and water buffalo. It seemed that all the men fished with nets, nightlines and with dynamite when they could procure it. Each night as we camped they would gather round and marvel at our spinners and plugs, rods and reels. Even our line and hooks were like gold-dust to them. It was all very sobering: I carried with me some £600 worth of tackle, which was nothing special for a trip of this sort, yet the average annual income of each village family might be a quarter of that figure. Yet, with so little, with their lives so hard, we were greeted everywhere with smiles and hospitality. We felt little like strangers each morning as village by village, men, women and children lined the beaches to wave us away and wish us well.

The Terrai plain was both heaven and hell. I lost a second big mahseer that simply ran out 150yd of line and carried on going. I saw several more large ones move and landed many small ones. I also began to see enormous catfish-potential as one swam under the raft and was so large that it actually lifted the craft and its five occupants bodily from the water. The wildlife was magnificent: we saw four tigers, snarling and free in the lush elephant grass that lined the river-banks. A rhinoceros appeared 5yd from us one evening and elephants came to drink at dawn and at dusk. There were crocodiles, wild boar, spotted and swamp deer; sambars, a mongoose, monkeys, pythons, peacocks, eagles, ospreys, kites, orioles, hornbills and jungle hens. The highlight for me was a Gangetic dolphin, one of perhaps only seven in the entire river system and, at that time, all believed to be miles south in India. I and the dolphin both fished the same pool for mahseer one boiling morning. We were so close that I could hear him breathe as he rose every minute or so, cutting a brown crescent through the water. At times I could see the sunlight wink in his eyes.

After all this it is sad and strange to talk of hell, of temperatures that soared to 120°F (48°C), of winds that rose to gale force and burned like a hairdryer, blasting sand into our hair, eyes and food. Forest fires erupted viciously and unpredictably and filled the air with smoke and ash. Joy developed a heat rash that covered her entire body in red irritating pimples and sores. We both had constant headaches. Our thirsts were unquenchable and the flies were impossible to escape from. Night provided relief, but then the jungle floor rustled with spiders and scorpions, and occasional storms flickered in the April sky. At least in November and February the climate is cooler and cleaner, the air purer and the fishing becomes even better.

A truly vast amount of water lies in western Nepal, most of it waiting to be explored, and its potential is hard to guess at. Remember, Himalayan mahseer are more sleek than the broad-shouldered, deep-bellied fish of southern India. I had always believed one of these former fish to be good at 15lb, big at 30lb and fabulous at 40–50lb. On the Terrai plains, I saw much bigger fish move and heard, reliably, of one that had been taken and eaten; its head alone weighed 25lb!

Catfish are at least as spectacular. There are many different varieties, of every outlandish colour, shape and size. The textbooks say that the largest of them grows to a ton!

Certainly, one specimen hooked with a night-line threatened to pull four entire families into the Karnali with it, so that they had to let go of the rope. The few and usually small catfish that I caught generally fell to spinners when I was mahseer fishing, but I felt sure that a bait in the deeper, slower pools would provide a memory of a lifetime.

Mahseer fact file

Seasons

The best time for mahseer varies according to the particular latitude. In Nepal the best months are probably November and February. Before November the monsoon has left the river still very high, while December and January tend to be fairly cold. February is a very pleasant month and the water is at a perfect level, but by March, especially later in the month the through April, the weather becomes tinder-dry as the monsoon of May/June approaches.

The Ganges mahseer demand critical timing. The traditional attack on them is mounted as soon as the monsoons peter out and the river begins to fall. During this

A small mahseer comes on to the gravels – all these fish are landed in this way

period the mahseer drop down from their spawning rivers, back into the Ganges itself and appear particularly vulnerable, especially at river confluences. The monsoon generally finishes around the end of August/beginning of September, so a trip should coincide with this period.

In the south the season is a little longer. The monsoons occur during our summer months but by late November or December the rivers begin to drop back to a fishable state. However, there is a degree of uncertainty about this and January and February appear to be the safest months. March is also good but the temperatures start to rise; April can produce fish if you can bear the extreme heat.

Passports and Visas

You must have entry visas when travelling to either Nepal or India. Application forms can be obtained from the High Commission of India, India House, Visa Section, The Aldwych, London, WC2B 4NA, or from the Royal Nepalese Embassy, Visa Section, 12A Kensington Palace Gardens, London W8 4QU. Postal applications take some time, so if possible it pays to collect the visas personally. Very often a tour operator will arrange this. It is useful to remember that visas for fifteen days can also be issued at Kathmandu airport and can be extended while you are in Nepal for a total of ninety days at an extra cost.

Baggage

At present, each angler is allowed 44lb of check-in baggage on international flights. In addition, you may take into the cabin with you a holdall which must fit in the overhead locker and a few smaller items like cameras or duty-free goods. Knives, scissors or any item that could be seen as an offensive weapon must not be carried in your hand-luggage and will be confiscated for the journey when your hand-luggage is checked. Once an item, which could be essential for the forthcoming fishing trip, is confiscated, it is sometimes a struggle to have it returned. Make sure that all baggage is very clearly labelled and that rods in particular are securely protected by a strong tube. You should carry your camera and films in your hand-luggage and be very careful with X-ray machines when you go through the security checks – a very few are old fashioned and not film safe.

Currency

The import and export of Indian and Nepalese rupees is forbidden. The exchange rate varies on a daily basis and inflation is high in most areas of Asia. However, as a rough guide there are now 35–40 Indian rupees to the pound and around 45–50 Nepalese rupees to the pound. On arrival in Delhi or Kathmandu, it is advisable to change some money into small denominations which are useful for tipping and paying taxis. You will find that the taxi-drivers never have change! Do not accept any torn or damaged notes as these will not be accepted by anyone else. Do remember to hold back the requisite airport departure tax that is required when flying out of Delhi, Bombay or Kathmandu. It would be very embarrassing to have spent all your money and not be able to leave the country! It is advisable to take traveller's cheques in small denominations and cash only small amounts of money at a time. It is a very complicated and time-consuming exercise to change rupees back to sterling, so this should be avoided if possible. Most international cedit cards are accepted in larger hotels, and shops and hotels will change traveller's cheques far more quickly than the average Asian bank.

Health

Although it is not a legal requirement to be inoculated to travel to India and Nepal, it is virtually essential to be vaccinated against cholera, typhoid, tetanus, meningitis and hepatitis. It is also wise to top up your polio immunisation. It is useful to carry certificates as proof of immunisations should they be required, although I have never been asked for them. Do note that if you have travelled within Africa during the past two years, you must carry to India proof of yellow fever inoculation. Malaria is present throughout lowland India and Nepal, especially in the more populated plains. Tablets can combat the disease and your doctor should be consulted before departure. Remember that malaria tablets need to be taken at least a week before leaving Britain. Stomach upsets are an ever-present problem, but can be avoided if you are careful, but not neurotic, about your diet. Never drink tap water unless it has been boiled and/or sterilised. Avoid food and unwashed fruit from the city bazaars. Local tea is virtually always safe but avoid drinks with ice-cubes in them. If you are going to fall sick, this will probably happen in the cities. Life in camps is generally fairly germ-free, so pay particular attention when you relax in that seemingly comfortable, safe hotel.

First-aid Kit

It is often useful to have with you a small personal first-aid kit. It should include: aspirins, antiseptic cream (such as Savlon), Elasto-plast, moleskin pads for blisters, medicine for diarrhoea relief (Lomotil and Imodium are both excellent), malaria tablets, insect repellent, sunburn barrier cream, lipsalve, water purification tablets, a 3in-wide crêpe bandage and safety-pins.

Clothing

It is easy to take too much clothing to Asia and it pays to take more fishing tackle and less in the way of underwear. Remember that it is possible to have clothes washed very cheaply virtually everywhere. Recommended would be 2 pairs of shorts and perhaps swimming trunks; 1 lightweight waterproof jacket; 2 pairs of light trousers or jeans; 1 pullover for areas where the evenings can be cool; 2 pairs of training shoes; 3 light shirts/tee-shirts; 3 pairs of light cotton socks and 3 changes of underwear. More specialised footwear is described on p108.

Miscellaneous Equipment

A sun-hat is essential for most people and sunglasses for everyone. A torch with spare batteries is invaluable and you will need reading matter for the flights and the possible long waits at station depots. Take a water bottle and, if possible, binoculars. The birds and wildlife can be exotic in the extreme. A light cotton sleeping-bag liner is also often a useful thing to take.

Photography

India and Nepal are a photographer's paradise and stunning photographs are virtually guaranteed. Generally I try to take a camera with wide, standard and telephoto lenses. Obviously, a zoom lens makes this job more compact. Lenses of 200mm never seem quite adequate; a 400mm lens is superior if you have one. Film of 64 ASA is excellent for most situations but obviously 200 or 400 ASA is required for longer lenses. Do not neglect black and white films which are excellent to pick out the 'character-full' life in the cities. Do respect the privacy of local people, especially in remote areas, and do not intrude unduly with your camera. Remember in particular that it is very impolite to photograph women or religious shrines. Take all your photographic needs with you; although you can buy films and even batteries in Asia, they are often expensive and out-of-date.

Tipping and Beggars

Tipping is a fact of life on the sub-continent. Outstretched hands and lingering hotel staff will be encountered with depressing regularity and often even junior officials expect some monetary reward. If a man has carried your bags or done some obvious service for you, a small tip of 5 or 10 rupees is the norm. Do not, however, tip taxi-drivers.

Once in the city and out of the hotel you are likely to be surrounded by hordes of beggars. Although it may seem heartless, it is vital to remain stony faced and to stride on. If you show indecision or shower rupees, you will simply be swamped. At many of the shrines there are some especially pitiful cases and there I feel it is up to the individual whether they melt or not. In the countryside try to avoid tipping wherever possible, but if you have made friends with locals, gifts of pens or fishing tackle are particularly appreciated.

Tackle for Mahseer

Mahseer are very large fish and their spirit equals their bulk. The rivers that they inhabit are also often breathtakingly wide and rapid, plunging frequently over huge boulders and monsoon-swept timbers. Under such circumstances it is hardly surprising that the odds are firmly on the side of the fleeing mahseer and, in fact, probably 50 per cent of the fish I have hooked myself or that have been hooked by others have escaped for one reason or another. To lose a big mahseer after a journey of thousands of miles can be at least as gut-wrenching an experience as dysentery itself and it is foolish not to take every single possible precaution with the tackle used.

Rods

Over the years I have broken three rods during mahseer battles and now I know that it makes sense to take only the most flawless weapons. Materials are important. The more modern carbon-fibre constructions are, of course, excellent in most conditions, but there are times when they will not stand up to the type of battering that they are bound to receive from a heavy fish in battle conditions. Probably better, or at least safer for the biggest fish in the wildest water, is a good, solid, hollow glass, type of rod. Whether carbon or glass is used, the test curve of a mahseer rod should not be less than 2lb and often 3lb or even 4lb is desirable. The rod should also be of a decent length – at least 11ft and possibly even 12ft. Too short a rod will not give you the necessary control over a fish weaving its way behind rocks and massive snags. The rod should also possess a gentle, all-through action so that it can cope with the sudden juddering plunges of the mahseer. Some anglers fish for mahseer with lighter tackle, but generally they live to regret it: when a mahseer beds itself to the river floor, using its huge pectorals like suction pads, a rod of real spine and substance is needed to get it on the move once more.

A lighter, more delicate rod is just acceptable for spinning. The ones that I use today are Peter Drennan Long Distance carp rods. These have a test curve of just over 2lb and are slightly over 12ft in length. They are light, precise and still have the spirit to deal with fish in excess of 50lb.

It is only sense to check every possible weak point on the rod. New eyes are essential if there is any doubt about the old ones. Check the ferrules for any possible cracks or imperfections. Ensure that the reel seating is totally secure.

Take care transporting the rod to Asia for if it is damaged in transit, then replacements will be impossible to find. It is highly unlikely that the airline will allow a rod to be taken on the plane as hand-luggage, so it is essential that the rod is secured in a very sound tube and is well labelled in case it is temporarily lost. A metal tube is superior to a plastic one as often a great deal of weight rests upon the rods in the hold.

Reels

For spinning, a large fixed-spool reel is adequate and I have no complaint whatsoever with my Shimano 4500 baitrunners over many months of Asian usage. These reels have a large line capacity, a smooth reliable clutch and a good back wind if necessary. Moreover, they are totally reliable and I have absolute confidence that they will not seize up during one of the marathon battles that take place in sweltering heat. Probably other big fixed-spool reels are as good, but it is essential that you have absolute faith in the tool that you take out there.

For bait work, where absolutely massive fish in excess of 80lb are expected, then it is probably wise to use a multiplier reel. The major reason for this is that they have enormous capacity and can take with ease 200yd or more or 40lb line. This astounding length can often be necessary: in February 1991 Steven Harper cast his ragi paste 80yd where it was picked up by a mahseer of over 100lb. The first run of this fish, before Steve could get to the boats, took off over 100yd of line. With a fixed-spool reel he would have been stripped; as it was, he could see the drum on his multiplier.

Take cloths, reel oils, spanners and screwdrivers with your reels: the work that they have to do is often gruelling. They can fall on sandy beaches, on stones or into the water. The heat is often baking and the fight is bound to test the gearing system to the full.

Lines

For lure fishing, lines of between 15 and 20lb breaking strain are probably adequate. There will be few occasions you will want to go under 15lb and spinning

with lines more than 20lb is often difficult and cumbersome. The acceptable norm is probably 18lb line.

For bait fishing, lines can be appreciably heavier: 25–40lb line is frequently used in the big pools of the rivers of southern India where fish can easily reach 80–90lb or more. In short, then, I generally take a range of line, including 15lb, 18lb, 20lb, 30lb and 40lb line. This covers virtually every eventuality.

Line is impossible to buy in Asia. For this reason it is essential to take all the line that you are likely to need with you. A lot of line is lost or damaged in fights and the normal casting over rocks and boulders takes its toll. On average, I have found it necessary to change the line every two to three days of intensive fishing.

Lures

Mahseer take both spoons and plugs and I

A selection of mahseer gear – the multiplier reel, the spinners, dead fish and the ragi paste

Mahseer fishing in the rapids really puts the pressure on tackle and man alike. Soon after this the author's rod broke on a big fish and he was forced to swim after the fleeing giant

have no idea which they prefer. In the south, locals appear to favour big silver spoons whereas on the Ganges most of the fish are caught on plugs. In Nepal both lures seem to score. I am reluctant to name particular makes and models of lure as I have only taken some fifty or sixty fish on artificials and very often I have not known why one type has succeeded rather than another. My experience has shown that constant experimentation can yield results. In general, I do like to use silver spoons as these catch the sun and glint it back

brightly. The size depends largely upon water conditions, but a good average would be a 3in spoon weighing around 1oz. Bigger spoons can prove irresistible in slightly cloudier water or for really enormous fish. There are, however, times when very small spoons – say, around 1in – appear to be the only ones effective. This was certainly the case in some Nepali rivers.

Most plugs are worth at least a cast or two. Yellows, browns and greens seem favourite colours and the most acceptable sizes are generally between 2 and 4in in length. Deep-diving plugs are often useful for picking out a fish in a pocket of water tucked behind a rock. A violent action is often irresistible. Shallow plugs really come into their own when working across the tail of a smooth glide just before it plunges into the rapids beneath. In short, it pays to take as wide a range of artificial lures as possible and to fish them with confidence, for any one could work on a particular day with a particular shoal of fish. Arguably, the most important aspect of the lure is not its shape, size, colour or action but the hooks with which it is armed.

Hooks

Without doubt, over the decades most mahseer that have come adrift have in some way bent or destroyed the hook. Virtually all freshwater hooks are useless for mahseer – it is as simple as that. For bait fishing with ragi or fish, it is probably best to use one of the large sea patterns made by Mustad. A piece of ragi paste is at least as large as a tangerine, so a large 6/0 hook is not anywhere near too immense. A selection of hooks from 3/0 to 6/0 is probably about right.

The lures are more difficult and probably the only possibility is to equip them with Partridge mahseer trebles. These were designed for Partridge by Paul Boote and are about as strong as any smaller trebles that I personally have come across. Sizes 4, 6 and 8 are probably adequate for most of your mahseer lure-fishing needs.

It is wise to take plenty of hooks on a long journey for they are not replaceable in Asia. Calculate how many you will need and then double that figure. It is frightening how many you can lose, not on fish alone but also on all manner of snags. Any hooks left over at the end of the trip are gratefully received by the Indians as presents and may well prove very useful to a remote village, often struggling for its very existence.

Weights

A large selection of weights is vital when bait fishing, to cope with the different sizes of paste and fish and the varying current speeds. Most typical continental weights will do, but the Indian trick is simply to hammer out a long sheet of lead and then twist it and nip it to the line above the hook. The perfect stuff to take for this business is a sheet of roofing lead. A piece about 1ft square should be enough for a journey and is easily cut into shape with sharp scissors.

General Accessories

Take a good assortment of large, strong, reliably built swivels. Two pairs of forceps are vital to remove deeply embedded hooks from the tough mahseer's mouth. Pliers are ueful to nip the lead to the line. Scissors serve all sorts of useful functions, especially when line of 30 or 40lb breaking strain is far too strong to snap or to cut with the teeth. A tape-measure is useful and if you like to use weights, scales will probably need to go to 112lb and the weigh sling must be correspondingly massive. It is a general rule in Asia to keep a mahseer for a while to let it recover after the fight. It is tethered to a tree or root by means of a soft rope tied through its gill flap. Take two or three 'stringers', each around 5yd long. Once a mahseer has been landed, your guide will ask first for the stringer and it is essential to have one with you in your pocket. Always take at least two torches with adequate batteries. These are not only useful for life in a tent where darkness falls quickly but also for fishing when trips start before dawn or go on long after sunset. For all but the toughest, a sun-hat is vital, but there is debate over the best sort of footwear. In the south, it has become traditional to wear hiking boots. The thinking is that these will protect the feet from the rocks, especially when a fish is on and has to be pursued. The problem is that hiking boots are difficult to transport and are heavy and hot to wear. In all probability, trainers serve just as well. Flip-flops and bare feet should be avoided. It is possible to pick up germs through cuts that come into contact with water and there is always the possibility of treading on a scorpion attracted by the waterside's dampness.

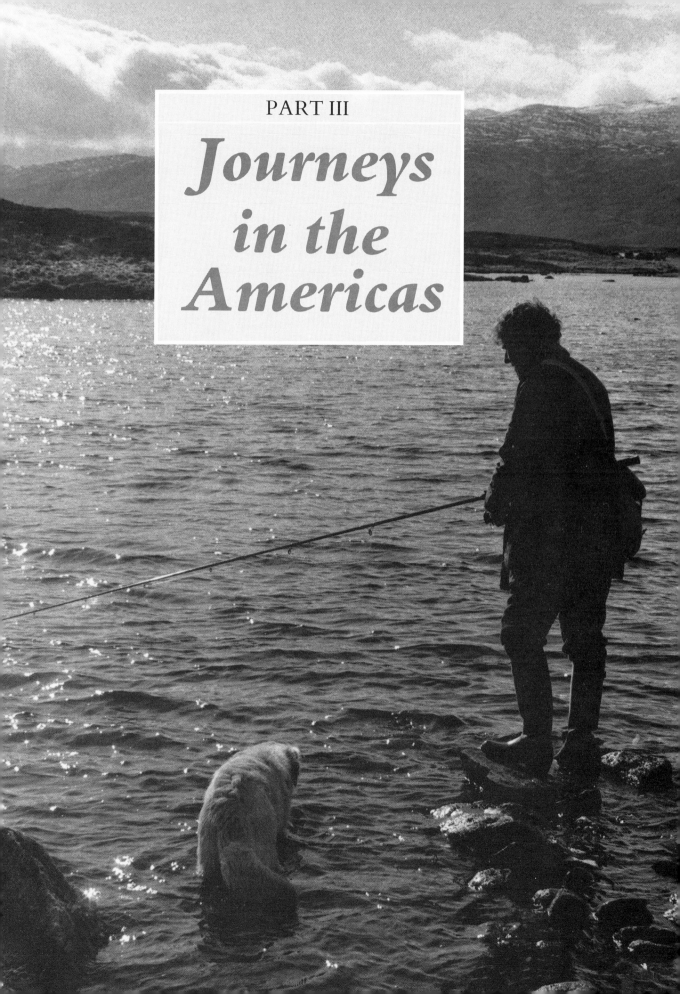

PART III

Journeys in the Americas

The North American Scene

It is a sad fact that a great deal of stereotyping goes on in angling: the coarse fisherman is seen as fat, tattooed and jam-sandwich eating. Equally, the salmon fisher is portrayed as tweedy, ex-army and generally alcoholic. Perhaps this is why angling in America has never really appealed to me – again, it is the stereotypes that we all see. I was influenced by those terrible films that are shown at the end of an angling dinner in which all the anglers wear shorts, kiss-me-quick hats and toothy grins. The fishing seems to be about short rods, cranked baits, shrieks of laughter and the senseless cudgelling of innumerable fish. The angler is invariably called Ed, the weather is invariably baking hot and the film is invariably booed off stage.

Of course, I realise now that American angling is far more than a badly directed film full of transatlantic wallies! In fact, the sport in America has a host of heroes – among them famous anglers like the great Lee Wulf who did so much to revolutionise salmon fishing this side of the Atlantic. And when

A very gaudy batch of steelhead flies

Fishing for char and salmon where the river meets the sea

you pick up modern American angling magazines, it is impossible not to realise that the sport is as fresh and alive in America as it was in the days of Negley Farson, Zane Grey and the other late greats. Who can deny the advances made by the trout fishermen of Montana, or the skills of the big-mouth-bass angler as he creeps along the creeks, dapping insects or little frogs? Who can question the ability and dedication of the predator anglers who hunt out the elusive muskies? And who cannot admire a man like Chris Batin whose list of trophy fish from Alaska is quite staggering?

Perhaps I have simply not known where to concentrate my attention or my energies. King salmon, silver salmon, sockeye salmon, pink salmon, chum salmon, lake trout, steelhead trout, rainbow trout, cut-throat trout, grayling, northern pike, tarpon, bonefish, large-mouthed bass, walleye, catfish – all these and a wealth of other tremendous creatures have meant that my eyes and my ambitions have swivelled around hopelessly without any real point of focus. This is so unlike Asia where the only real gamefish is the mahseer, or Africa where tigerfish and Nile perch rule the roost. In fact, this book could easily have been about the sports fish of America pure and simple.

So I had to choose what in my heart I would really love to do across the Atlantic and I decided on Canada. Labrador sounded entrancing, the total wilderness experience, fishing for bright, silver salmon that demand an active, positive approach from the angler. Then there are the steelheads: like many other anglers I have caught many tired stillwater rainbow trout, stale from the stewponds, ragged of fins. Despite their inauspicious start to life, these fish still battle all the way to the net and many is the time that I have wondered what their mighty sea-running cousins are like. If these small, sad apologies for fish could fight like this, what could the real rainbows be like?

The Labrador Experience

Wild fishing is what Labrador is about and Shirley Deterding explains its appeal:

I love wilderness fishing – Labrador and Alaska are the two remaining wild places left on Earth for the salmon. Of the two, I prefer Labrador as the fish are Atlantic salmon rather than the red sockeye which do not fight as well. After all my visits to North America I can safely say that my favourite place is Michael's river about a one-and-a-half hour flight in a float plane from Goose Bay. It takes two days to reach this remote and lovely place. You take a plane from Heathrow to St John's in Newfoundland. After an overnight stay, you move on again by air to Goose Bay in Labrador on a scheduled flight of about two hours. Then if you are lucky with the weather, for the fog closes in at a moment's notice, and if there is a float plane available, you are off again to this northern outpost. As you drone in at about ninety-five miles an hour in a single-engine Otter float plane over the tundra, its wild beauty makes you realise that there must be miles of Earth that no human foot has ever trodden on. The camp is approached flying along the river, where, even in August, there is still snow lying on the banks down to the water's edge. You realise what it is like in winter when the snow piles high, even to the very chimney-pots of the cabin you are looking at now and when the temperatures sink to minus forty and anything plastic will shatter if touched.

Now you are taxiing towards a jetty by the log cabin that is situated on a spit of land between the long strip of white sand on the ocean's edge and the river. It is all unbelievably beautiful. On a clear day, the icebergs drift into the bay with accompanying whales and seals and the clear aquamarine-blue sea is covered with an endless variety of wild duck, snow geese, eiders, loons and multitudes of small shoreline birds that dazzle in the bright air.

Fishing is a magnificent experience and often you can travel up-river to try the many and varied pools in a native Indian-built boat. The only difference between today's boat and those of centuries ago is the electric motor pushing you up the current. Bears, moose and caribou can be sighted. Wolves come down shyly to drink from the river. Ospreys, fish eagles and long-eared owls can be sighted hunting and fishing up-river for anything small that strays into the shallows. Here is a peace and tranquillity long forgotten in these busy islands of our own. There is no sight or sound of aeroplanes or machines apart from the drone of our own outboard motor. At lunchtime a fire is built on the riverside and a small grilse is skilfully cooked for you by your Indian guide and you will eat it as fresh as it comes from the frozen waters. A grey jay, known to the locals as a 'Whisky Jack', will come and sit on your hand and be fed bits of bread or fish skins while other small birds busy themselves in the branches of the tall thin fir trees, making the most of the short summer they have available before flying south again.

Most of the run of fish are grilse but large salmon come upstream too. I was lucky once to hook such a fish on my first day. It was before dawn when I left the warmth of the log cabin to face the cool winds blowing off the ice but there was an incoming tide which could just bring success. I walked the sand, fresh marked by bear, wolf and caribou, and watched whales feeding in the bay as the sun rose. My light rod and small single-hooked fly looked puny against the might of the bay but I kept working and finally found some success. The fish fought wildly and bravely and at one time it jumped clear of the water and landed on the far bank in its mad effort to get free of my hooks. Then it careered two or three pools down-stream towards the sea with me running through the water trying to keep contact. Eventually, after about twenty minutes, the fish was circling deep before me and I managed to raise it in the water where my guide Russ managed to put the net underneath it. It was sixteen pounds and glinted silver and was covered in sea lice.

The fish in Labrador fight twice as hard as Scottish salmon and they seem to snatch the fly rather than take it in the usual leisurely way. They will scream yards of line off the reel, spending more time in the air than in the water, and it all makes for the most exciting fishing that I know.

A perfect example of a salmon from Labrador

Steelheads

After two years or sometimes more of stream life, steelhead parr begin their down-river journey to the sea. At this time increased activity of the thyroid gland makes the small fish lose their markings and adopt a silvery sheen. They are now technically smolts. Most young fish adapt to the sea water, although this depends to some degree on how long they have been in fresh. Steelheads spend between several months and up to four years at sea before returning to the streams of their birth to spawn. Some fish come up in the spring and some in the autumn and this difference seems to be genetically controlled. There is, still, a great deal that is not yet known about the steelhead's biology. Certainly those of the Skeena river system do seem to be markedly superior to many other fish, but for what reasons nobody can be quite sure. Perhaps it is something to do with water, genetics or food quality – many theories have been passed around over the years without any solid conclusions being reached. What is quite certain is that for many years

An aerial shot of the Skeena river system

This is what it's all about! Richard Gibbs cradles a superb male fish

Fishing in the snow and the cold

writers have eulogised about the steelhead's sporting qualities. Christopher Battin in *How to Catch Alaska's Trophy Sport Fish* describes his own experience:

> Steelheads are the nomads of the rainbow clan. From their swaggering jaunts in the Pacific Ocean, they acquire a wildness that large stream or river rainbow stocks never attain. Steelheads are the sportfish of superlatives. They intrigue and challenge the mind. An angler – muscles strengthened from a summer of fighting large salmon – finds his physique diminished to an exhausted, often times quivering mass of flesh after battle with a steelhead. Such a fish wins either by only its freedom, or more often than not, by breaking loose of its air-slashing aerobatics and powerhouse runs . . .
>
> I remember a wilderness foray after steelheads several years ago. Darkness was fast approaching, along with the cold of a lingering winter night. I'd been steelhead fishing most of the day and I was dead tired. However, the continuous casting and concentration usually associated with this type of fishing weren't what produced my aching muscles. Rather, I was experiencing the towering effects of battling steelheads all day long. For this kind of fatigue most fishermen would gladly trade the secret location of their favourite fishing holes. The only thing that prevented me from fishing myself into an unconscious euphoria was the rapidly receding daylight. Proceeding to drift my line through the dark indigo pool, I felt my line hesitate momentarily. It was a familiar sensation. My tired arms instinctively jerked upwards in a sweeping arc and though darkness had completely overtaken the area, I could hear an enraged steelhead's response: a series of resounding splashes. Memories of the day's earlier steelhead aerobatics flashed through my mind in lieu of the battle I could't now witness.
>
> The steely ran through its manoeuvres and eventually submitted itself stubbornly to my constant pressure. I slowly followed the line to the fish's mouth. In the blackness I gently unhooked what I estimated to be an eight-pound fish, still ice-cold from the depths. After releasing my fish, I dragged myself back to the tent camp a few hundred yards downstream. Suddenly, as if someone had lit a match, the eerie glow of the Northern Lights burst into long streamers radiating across the northern sky. It was a fitting and proper way to end a wilderness trip for such a remarkable game fish.

In *A River Never Sleeps*, Roderick Haig-Brown writes about the day he caught a large steelhead:

> January, 1929, was a cold month on Vancouver Island. One cold windy Sunday I took the skiff and poled up into the Canyon Pool. Snow began drifting in coldly from the North and the line kept freezing in the rings of the rod. After half-an-hour of it my fingers were so cold and stiff that I

could hardly turn the reel to bring the bait in. I thought of going home but made another cast instead and hunched down into my mackinaw to watch the swing of the ice-hung line as the rod top followed the bait around. The fish took with a jolt that snapped the ice fragments yards away. He ran straight upstream, deep down, jumped as he was opposite me and fell back on his tail. My stiff fingers fumbled wildly to recover line and failed miserably – only the drag of the current on the belly of the line kept a strain on him. A moment later I was trying as frantically to find the drum of the reel and check his heavy run to the tail of the pool. I had the feeling that a big fish in his first runs should give one a feeling of temporary help-lessness, of being a little late for every move he makes, dependent on a break of luck to reduce his strength until it is evenly matched to the strength of the tackle. This fish seemed determined to run right on out of the pool and down the rapids, and my only hope was to follow him in the skiff. I began to run and stumbled towards it over the difficult icy footing. Then he jumped again, just above the rapids. Without help from me he turned and held almost still in five or six feet of heavy water. I tightened on him gently, and began to walk slowly backwards to where I'd hooked him. He came, slowly and quietly, and from then on I had a measure of control.

He kept me busy for ten or fifteen minutes after that. I filled my boots with icy water, stumbled after him, checked his rushes, watched his jumps and at last brought him close enough to set the gaff. He was clean and beautiful, so strongly marked with deep water colours that he might have been caught in salt water. And he weighed twenty-two pounds, the only steelhead of over twenty pounds that I've ever yet caught.

There was snow in the grey evening air and a biting wind snarled along the Babine river as Richard Gibbs decided to fish a last run for the day. The water in front of him was wide, shallow, rapid and bitingly cold and he was numbed through to the bone after a gruelling day of mental and physical activity. He cast long, his fly rode high in the water and in the falling light it was just possible to see a bulge 30yd from him. It was impossible not to feel the rush of the hooked fish. There is no point in describing again the fight of a fresh-run steelhead under snow-laden clouds: suffice to say that once experienced it is never forgotten, nor the sight of the beaten fish. Richard just looked at it lying against the snow. It was simply absolutely perfect.

Of course it went back. That is the wisdom of the Americans these days. A very few fish are kept to eat on the bankside or perhaps as the occasional trophy, but the majority are returned to the rivers to swim away free, spawn, and even return to the sea to renew their life-cycle. In Britain we have a lot to learn about this philosophy and catch and release is still struggling to make a foothold here. There are arguments against the policy and some of them are sound, but in the face of declining aquatic environments it is hard to cling blindly and obstinately to old habits and customs. The American way must be the one of the future and the time must come when we all follow it.

Richard Gibbs prepares to release a superb fish

I have not yet fished for steelhead, but I will – I must. Talking to Richard Gibbs about steelhead is a heart-stopping experience for any angler. His descriptions of the river, the forests around and the crackling log fires in the cabins at night are inspirational. He shows you his box of flies – great, gaudy things that would look better decorating a Christmas tree – and you can imagine them pulsing through the dark Canadian rivers in the fall, glinting that fatal moment and hooking into the jaw of a wild fish.

A close-up of two steelhead flies. The top one is designed to skim on the surface

This weird creation is meant for steelheads – part fly, part spinner and part bait

Canada fact file

Seasons

Canada is a vast area with great geographical and climatic differences between north and south, east and west. Therefore to describe all the seasons and fishing available to the angler would be far too great a task even to contemplate. All I can do therefore is to concentrate on these two areas of excellence: salmon and trout fishing in Labrador and the steelhead runs of the Skeena river system in British Columbia. In Labrador, fishing starts when the ice melts from the rivers, generally around mid to late June. Char are among the first fish to run once the rivers are free, along with the larger salmon. Probably the prime time on most Labrador rivers is in June, for in August the smaller male salmon and grilse tend to follow on behind. On many rivers the hot period, when fish are really flooding in, is relatively brief, often only two to three weeks in length, but all this is related to how far north the river is situated and it is imperative to get accurate local advice. Most of the fishing in Labrador is done around the estuary mouth, but it is possible to increase the season by moving up-river to a wilderness lodge where the salmon can be again encountered close to their spawning beds. It must be said, though, that the most active and fresh fishing is closer to the sea. In September the fishing slows down but, as on many British rivers, often a late run of some very large fish comes through.

The season for steelheads in British Columbia is much more open-ended, but on the Skeena/Babine system September, October and early November are favoured months. In September the water is still warm and most of the fishing takes place on the surface with flies. There is often not a great head of fish in the rivers at this time and October sees more fish moving up-river. The fishing still tends to be on the surface, but a sinking-tip line is often an asset. October on this river system is probably the prime time as the cool nights clear the water perfectly. Late in October and running into November is certainly the period for the biggest trophy fish. The weather cools down appreciably and more very large fish pass through, stacking up behind the salmon that have already passed. However, all this is generalised and what should happen; there is still doubt about much of the steelhead lifestyle and

the experts, even on the rivers themselves, can still be puzzled by their behaviour.

Tackle

In Labrador, salmon fishing is very similar to our own on wide, broad, shallow rivers. In fact, the salmon gear that suits you at home on the Spey or the Tay will do very nicely in Labrador. There is a growing preference for lighter tackle which allows a more delicate presentation and probably a greater thrill in the fight. Long casting is seldom vital and the key to good fishing is to wade, cover water close to you and keep the flies active and dancing near the upper layers. Labrador salmon fishing is a very active, 'on your toes' type of sport and fishing light helps this approach immensely.

There are various ways of fishing for the steelhead, but the British angler will find something among all the options that suits him nicely. Try a 10ft reservoir rod or a single-handed salmon rod. A floating line is excellent, with just perhaps a faster sink-tip in October. Surface flies work excellently and they are frequently tied in the pattern of a muddler head. Often big bristles are glued on to increase the bow-wave that the fly gives off. This is particularly exciting fishing and the steelhead can be seen powering in to the fly dragging across the current. For general flies the larger versions of our own reservoir lures in many varied colours are excellent. Also, the locals often use flies that are made to look like the salmon eggs upon which the steelheads feed.

A good deal of spinning with copper and silver spoons also goes on for steelhead. And there is bait-fishing, too! This is often carried out with 'corkies' – coloured beads made to imitate salmon eggs. Two are placed on the line, sometimes the top one even carrying little propeller blades to make it spin and dance. The hook is set below the bottom bead, often with a little wool around its shank to catch in the steelhead's teeth and make early rejection more difficult. 'Corkies' can be fished just like worms with the lead up-front or they can even be drifted down-river under a float.

Clothing

In Labrador the saying goes that 'if you don't like the weather, wait half-an-hour and it will change'. For this reason take wet-weather clothing, along with shirts and even a pullover or two. Chest-waders are an advantage to reach the prime spots, but thigh-waders will adequately serve for most stretches of the river. Steelhead fishing often takes place during severe cold, so it makes sense to take as much warm clothing as possible. It is important to wear chest-waders with plenty of thermal underwear beneath.

Health Considerations

Labrador should present very few dangers of any real description. Although bears are common, this is a true wilderness area and the wildlife tends to be very discreet. It is a remote area where the whales swim just offshore and amid the icebergs and it is often difficult to appreciate that you are not alone. Do not leave fish on rocks to pick up later for almost certainly an otter, mink or bear will steal it. The midges can be vicious but are not generally as voracious in mid-river or near the coast where a breeze usually keeps them away. However, any exploration into a wooded area on a muggy day with little breeze can be interesting, to say the least!

By comparison, British Columbia has generally a softer climate and black bears and grizzlies are everywhere. Obviously, if the angler treats these with respect, there should be little danger from the animals. Do take care, however, when going outside the hut at night for often these animals forage very close to humanity. A British angler should realise that on the Skeena river system there will be dying salmon all around him. This can be something of a shock when the sight of a single salmon in Scotland with UDN is enough to spoil the day. However, this is the natural life-cycle of these fish and one we must accept. The worst is often in September when the still, warm weather and the dead bodies can render the banks far from sweet.

Stars of South America

With so many species swimming the huge river systems of South America it is hard to know where to start looking for the greatest challenges. In effect, however, for the sport fisherman there are very definite places to start – for instance, with the dorado.

Earlier this century the Upper Parana river in Brazil around the beautiful Falls of Iguassu was considered to be the finest dorado territory. This is the area described by J. W. Hill in his book *The Golden River*. Hill was Financial Secretary to the Treasury in England and was a member of the famous Houghton Club and an acknowledged master on the River Test. However, dorado captured his attention and imagination like no other fish:

> No one who has fished for both salmon and dorado will dispute that the first rush of a dorado is far stronger than that of a salmon of the same size. It is faster, longer and heavier. It is like nothing else in the world. Before you have time to think, one hundred yards have whizzed off your reel and the great fish is rushing first in one direction and then another, hurling himself out of the water, crashing back into it with a bang and shaking himself in mad fury at his restraint. That is true and it is all in favour of the dorado. But the salmon has the advantage in one point. He has more resource; for he can fight in stillwater as strongly as in swift. To sum up, however, I consider the dorado the gamer fish. The first few minutes of a big one give you more than you get in salmon fishing and, pound for pound, he is stronger and more muscular.

The dorado captured the imagination of many, including L. J. McCormick, who describes his experience in *Fishing Around the World*:

> At intervals we discussed dorado; what a fine and sporting game fish it was to prove, possessing, as we found, the two important qualities which some authorities insist on for a true gamefish – that is: active, intelligent resistance to the angler's wiles, and subsequent culinary satisfaction. The dorado we sought (*Salminus maxillosus*) is one of four varieties which are in no way related to *Salmo salar*. Its large scales are burnished brightly to a wonderful old gold tone, and, to add to its splendour, its fins are of brilliant scarlet orange. Across the caudal fin runs a black vertical stripe providing a final note of elegance to the fish's powerful and robust body. For colour there is no doubt that the dorado yields to no river fish, but its

A great catch of dorado taken in the early years of this century

form does not quite equal in design the streamline of a salmon. It is this stockiness of build, however, which accounts for its superior strength. The dorado has an immense mouth, considering the fish's trim appearance, and one is always somewhat surprised to see its huge gape when opened. Within there is a series of short but powerful teeth, set like a ripsaw in a single even row. Dorado have been captured up to some fifty pounds in weight and it is probable that sixty pounds is their limit.

The dorado fights to the last ounce. It jumps well and frequently it shakes its head and tries to throw the spoon, but it is fairly easy to hook as its mouth is not bony inside. If the fish is hooked at all firmly it will probably be captured unless the tackle breaks. The dorado is a predacious fish, feeding on smaller fish which it catches by speed swimming.

The dorado is an extremely game fish and lies in swift water. Not for him the still pools. Upstream from a big rock where the water divides, or just in the eddy of a horetail below, he is found. Generally he prefers water three feet deep, where he can make a lightening dash for some small fish – his prey.

But above all challenges, South America can offer the arapaima. This is the largest wholly freshwater fish in the world and can measure at least 8ft. Not only is it large but it is also fascinating to look at and fights, apparently, like no other fish. It also happens to be probably the rarest fish in the world and inhabits the most remote parts of some of the most inhospitable places on earth. L. J. McCormick described this outstanding fish:

The arapaima is startling not only because of its size but also for its colour. The fish has a long body, almost cigar shaped, that is covered with large olive-green scales which shade from the very dark on the back to very light on the belly. Beginning about half-way along the body these scales are tinged at the rear edges with a vivid red hue which suffuses them more and more until towards the tail they have become almost entirely scarlet. The shape of the fish, when one has become used to it, will appear completely logical. First one feels that it is too long for its girth, but in point of fact the arapaima is well proportioned and weighs more per inch than one would be led to suppose.

A certain amount is known about the habits of the arapaima. It seems that they rarely inhabit water deeper than 16ft and frequently they prefer the shallower margins covered in reeds where small fish live. It seems that an arapaima will have its favourite beat and will often patrol an area of water day after day – an area often a mile or so in length. One of their habits is to splash on the surface and this is probably done to flush small fish from the weeds to where they can be attacked. When this happens, the head does not come clear and all the angler sees is the tail with the dorsal and anal fins which function as a unit, slapping the water, making a great noise and stirring up the mud and the silt. This type of behaviour makes them particularly vulnerable to the Indians, who move out in their canoes and sit for long periods of time with their spears until an arapaima displays itself close to them. This approach is said to work for anglers. The trick is to cover water, looking hard for that flash of red arapaima tail and then to get as close as possible before casting a fish bait close to it. Obviously, to fish blind in such huge sheets of water is to court failure and for this reason the dry season is considered to be the best time to hunt these incredible creatures.

The size that arapaima can reach is somewhat vague and writing this book in England has been a distinct disadvantage as there is very limited information or research material available. Also, in the past a great deal of eye-witness report has been vague or inaccurate. It seems that it has been all too easy to over-estimate this very strange and exciting fish.

In the earlier part of this century an angler named McTurk described his experience of arapaima as follows:

I'm inclined to think that the average size of an arapaima is between six feet six inches and seven feet six inches, but now and again some are caught which are considered freaks as they are very thick for their length and would therefore weigh above the average of fish that long, or else they are very thin and long for their girth and occasionally one is come across that is very much larger than the average, although it may be said to be properly shaped.

The largest fish that McTurk ever landed was speared and was 9ft long. This fish probably weighed somewhere between 400 and 450lbs, somewhat more than the average which is probably around 150–250lb for a full-grown fish. Obviously, there are very likely to be larger fish living in the Amazon or some of the other mighty Latin American rivers and possibly talk of the 600-, 700- or 800-pounders is well founded. Equally obviously, any arapaima landed during a fishing trip to such wild, huge, inhospitable places is an achievement, whatever its size.

Very few accounts of successful rod and line fishing for arapaima exist. One journey was, however, successful and in September 1913, a party led by Sir Walter Egerton, with two rods angling at a time, succeeded in catching seven of these fish in two-and-a-half hours. This great event took place in a deep pool on the Simoni, a small tributary of the River Rupununi. Apparently, tarpon rods were used and the hooks were tied on to piano-wire leaders. Chunks of fish-meat were the bait, measuring about 2½in square and the fish took these almost immediately. Each arapaima gave an excellent fight, many jumped and many times fish got away by head-shaking and throwing the hooks. The largest of them landed in that particular session weighed an amazing 200lb and was just short of 7ft long with a girth of just over 3ft. The angler had to take to the boat and he was pulled up and down the pool with two guides for many minutes. Another fish, estimated at around 300lb, broke away after a long fight.

Martin James – the bravest of all anglers – holds a huge Amazon catfish

Catfish come in all shapes and sizes. Here Johnny Jensen holds one caught from the deep south of India

Amazon Journey

Martin James, the angling presenter for Radio 5 and Radio Lancashire, is one of the most remarkable anglers I have ever met and certainly one of the greatest adventurers. His life has been one long experience both before and after he contracted the debilitating disease multiple sclerosis.

In his younger days, before MS struck, Martin made sixteen journeys to the Amazon Basin. The place mesmerised him and drew him back again and again, for it held a mysterious fascination for him ever since he had read about it in *Boy's Own* magazine in the 1940s. The variety of the waters in this jungle wilderness intoxicated the young angler: two thousand species as opposed to a hundred and fifty or so in Europe. There were piranha, of course, and although they are not nearly as dangerous as legend would have it, the natives who accompanied Martin would cut off the fish's bottom jaw before they would take out the hook and eat their catch. There were lulkani, hard-fighting fish around 8lb that Martin could fish for on the fly. Whenever possible, Martin liked to get out his fly rod but there would be always a need for a wire trace even with a fairly small fly; few fish in jungle waters are without teeth, apart from one like a naze and another like a barbel. The fish that really excited Martin were the innumerable catfish species that were so important to the Indian diet. For them Martin used 12ft beach-casters (he remembers the Abu Atlantic being the tool) with an Abu Ambassador 7000 multiplier loaded with a 30lb line. The dorado catfish, with a mouth like the Mersey Tunnel, was the most cherished prize. The trick was to catch a 5lb catfish, chop it in two and load the bait with big sea-hooks. Dusk was the time that the catfish came out, when there would be a million insects biting and stinging and the sights and sounds of the jungle would be magnificent. The Equatorial sunsets were blindingly beautiful and it is easy to imagine Martin sitting in a boat, in these enormous sleeping rivers, held in position by an ever-paddling Indian. For three or four hours, well into darkness, the boat would not move an inch as angler and guide chatted quietly in the darkness. The reel would click, then go wild and the canoe would veer up and down the river, at times totally out of control before the power of the fish. Frantic paddling, the water thrashing, the reel screeching, shouting, instructions, and then, at last, exuberant cheering: the village would have food for a day or more!

Sometimes the reel clicked, the rod bowed and the canoe was towed by something completely different: after only a few seconds the inky waters of the Amazon would part and yards away from Martin and guide a great salmon-pink dolphin would rise out of the water. The line would break like cotton as all 3 tons of it crashed back and the canoe would rock to the waves. The Indians there revered the dolphins and believed that the spirits came back to the world in their form. Martin would relax and laugh, turn to his guide and say 'There goes your grandfather!'

There cannot be more dangerous places in the world to fish than the Amazon Basin and it is hard to know where to start cataloguing the potential perils. Martin talks of the big stingrays that lie in the sand in the shallow water, a lethal menace to anyone getting out of a boat or simply dipping to wash. Then there are the carnero – minnow-sized fish but still killers. Apparently, they can swim up the urine of a man relieving himself in the river, enter the penis and eat away at his insides. For this reason the natives wear cane sheaths around their private parts.

Everything in this wilderness is exotic or enormous. Ahead of you an anaconda can be hanging from a tree, a snake of well over 20ft in length. The butterflies dance around like gaily coloured saucers and the parrots swarm in their squawking thousands. The river itself is totally untamable and Martin has seen it rise 38ft in a few hours. Whole villages would disappear and the bank would break away in colossal pieces of 5 or 6 acres which would bob down-river towards the sea like so many floating islands.

All over the world fish have been caught in the most ingenious of ways. Here a fishing cormorant is being prepared for battle

Arapaima Adventure

Keith Elliot is the angling correspondent for *The Independent* and for *The Field*. He typifies the modern thinking angler who also does a great deal of travelling. He has already visited remote parts of Russia with that other great angler Fred Buller and is now contemplating a quest in search of the record great white shark with Vic Sampson (the shark, they believe, is approaching 30ft long and could weigh as much as 7,000lb – considerably bigger even than the notorious Jaws!) But it was his journey to the Amazon in search of the arapaima that interested me: this is a story of great interest to anybody planning a campaign to Latin America or to anywhere particularly demanding. Keith described his experience as we sat on a bleak River Kennet one cold day. These are his words as I remember them:

Our decision was to try for arapaima on a tributary of the Amazon that flows through Ecuador. The reasoning behind Ecuador was that we knew it was a safer country than either Peru or Brazil and it is one thing to fight the wildlife and the temperatures but quite another to struggle with drug cartels, soldiers or simply bandits! I like to think that we planned the trip meticulously. There were six of us in all and we were careful to have a good character mix and to take anglers with a great deal of experience. There was, for example, Vic Sampson who is world renowned for catches of giant sea fish, but there were also very skilled carp anglers as well – really a lot of men with a lot of experience of big fish. Obviously, we all had the necessary injections and took a great deal of medicines but we also paid for one of our party to have a complete first-aid course – this way we would be ready if anything went wrong in the jungle miles from a hospital.

We flew into Quito, which is at just over nine thousand feet and made for a hotel where we found beds for a dollar each per night! The plan was then to bus it to our chosen stretch of river but when we saw the conditions of travel in the buses of Ecuador we quickly changed our minds. In the end we hired a lorry to take us and the equipment into the jungle – haggling took quite a while and even then we didn't get things quite right. In actual fact, after some 20 miles we came back and started all over again! It's a good idea in these sorts of places if you get the exact figures very well sorted out before the deal is clinched.

Anyway, the journey only lasted for twelve or thirteen hours and on the way we had eight punctures! Fortunately the lorry had a good dozen spares so we weren't caught out badly – apart from losing a fair bit of time.

A faded photograph of an angler fast into a big fish in the jungle. The arapaima is probably the rarest fish in the world and certainly the greatest challenge known to any freshwater fisherman

Right at the end of the road – and I do mean the end of the road – we met our guide, Fernando. The town itself was in the fringes of jungle and pretty unsophisticated. The hotel wasn't one we wanted to spend a great deal of time at and we got our tackle together quite quickly and prepared to move off. Excitement by now was running high. The guide had got for us two motorised canoes and as soon as possible these were packed with all the gear we thought we would need and we were motoring down the river. That second night we stayed in a hut belonging to one of Fernando's friends. I say a hut! All it was really was four poles stuck into the ground with banana leaves thrown over for a roof. There was an upstairs approached by a ladder where you had to go to escape the ants as darkness fell. The mosquitoes were absolutely horrendous so I slept in my bag, preferring the desperate heat to the damage I would otherwise face. In fact, one man who slept near-naked was bitten 189 times on a single leg! The next days were spent travelling, moving slowly towards our planned destination. The river was very much in flood which worried us. Our plans had been made on the assumption that it would be low water and now we found that the climate had gone against all our expectations.

At last we made another village, occupied by a tribe who, we understood, still made a sacrifice once a year! Now a lagoon lies behind this village and we were told that arapaima existed in there. We fished quite hard and took a lot of fish, including some very odd ones indeed, many of which we didn't have any idea of naming. What we really needed was a detailed book to give us some clues, so it is quite possible that some could have been species not officially detailed before. Most of them were fish up to about a pound and generally of the catfish family. Most of them again had teeth of some sort or another.

We spent some time at the village without any sightings of arapaima at all and then decided it was time to move on to what was considered a very 'hot' area. So it was into the boat again and off once more on the river. A certain amount of boredom was creeping in because so far we were seeing very little wildlife. True, we did catch a deer swimming for its life and the more squeamish ones among us prevailed upon its release instead of its destiny for the cook-pot. Then, at last, we left the main river and moved into the Tiputini National Park. This area is patrolled by the army as it is close to the border with Peru and is a disputed area. We had to give up our passports which was nerve-racking and promise to obey the various rules. Army or not, they were obviously doing the wildlife some good because now we began to see freshwater dolphin, giant turtles, giant kingfishers of all sorts and literally clouds of parrots. We really did believe that we were in the heart of the jungle now and excitement, having dipped, began to rise at once.

Fernando took us to the home of his brother, or friend – we never really did fathom out which – and this was our base. It was right on the river and we were told that we were deep in arapaima country. Here, though, we could see the full extent of the high water and it was certainly twenty feet more than we had bargained for. It was right up the trees and often only the tips were visible.

A little way from the base was the lagoon that had been our objective all along. Getting there was a nightmare and we had to hack through pretty solid jungle. There were giant ants that fell on us and, believe me, really chewed hunks from our arms and legs. But no matter, the lagoon was absolutely everything we had hoped for. It was around four or five acres and we were told that no white man had ever been there before. It was very easy to believe. We wanted to fish at once and we anchored against the trees as some of the party tried to catch fish to use as bait. This had been a major problem all along: we had expected the waters to teem with small fish but this actually was not the case and catching anything bait size was very hard work. Fortunately, I had packed some size 16 hooks and baiting with paste meant that we did catch some tiny catfish and something that looked like a cross between a sprat and a shad. We decided to take it in turns to fish for bait and to fish for arapaima.

That first trip we put out some dead fish on three rods and I had brought with me some cans of luncheon meat and put a large chunk on one of my rods. It had not been in the water for long when the float went under and a big fish moved doggedly off into the centre of the lagoon. Suddenly there was nothing. The line had been bitten right through and it made us realise that wire traces would be pretty well essential.

What we began to catch were piranha – around three to four pounds – all armed with the most serious-looking teeth. In fact, one bit through a forged hook! So bad did those teeth look that we had to kill them before handling. We didn't want to kill for the sake of it, so we tried to cook and eat the piranha and they were absolutely disgusting. We also tried piranha for bait, but the only fish that seemed to like piranha were piranha, so even that had to be given up.

Although the lagoon looked absolutely perfect, the rise in the river level had really ruined it for us. It was well over twenty feet deep and we had been expecting somewhere between three and six. Also, it was coloured like deep, dark mud. This meant that we could not locate anything. We did, however, see some enormous swirls and once, just once, saw an arapaima turn. This in some ways was the absolute highlight of the entire journey. We saw its tail fin and its dorsal quite clearly and we were absolutely wild with excitement. At other times we heard enormous splashes, especially at night, so we couldn't see what fish were responsible. But, believe me, there was some excitement being generated.

Obviously we tried fishing at night and one good thing about this was that the piranha switched off totally after dusk. Night fishing produced two serious runs and two very big fish hooked. The trouble was that we could not see the snags but the fish knew exactly where they were and both we lost. Whether they were arapaima or not is difficult to say, but our feeling at the time was that they were very large cats.

Masses of problems emerged. One problem with Fernando was that for a long time he thought that we wanted to see him catch an arapaima himself with a spear and this, of course, was a pretty serious misunderstanding! The next thing was that we found we couldn't fish tied up to trees. The ants simply poured down on to us and devoured us. The trees themselves were covered with spikes and the heat meant that we just couldn't wear a lot of clothes.

Naturally, there was tension over the bait. Nobody wanted to miss out on the proper fishing and spend the whole day catching tiddlers. There were a lot of efforts made to use inferior baits which obviously jeopardised the success of the expedition.

We also had some pretty narrow escapes! This was primary jungle and unlike anything any of us had ever seen. Fernando kept stressing to us that the jungle was very, very dangerous and he would only allow us to go out with him accompanying. We even accompanied each other on trips to the loo! Sometimes Fernando took us out on something like a school nature walk and everywhere there were green tree frogs and birds of all shapes, sizes and colours. It was a tragedy that we did not have the wildlife books with us to really analyse the dozens of species we saw. On one particular occasion Fernando collected some ants for us and asked that we eat them. They tasted of lemon! Then he dug up some roots that tasted just like chocolate. We were still eating this root when he pulled us to one side and motioned us back into the jungle. In a clearing ahead of us, on the ground lay what looked like a very large stick. In fact it was a ferdelance – one of the most dangerous snakes in the world and the only snake to actually chase! Fernando crept up on it, although we didn't think he should try at the time, and killed it with a stick. It was around 9ft long and Vic Sampson put it round himself and said that he was going to take it back, skin it and use it for a belt. Soon we were back in the camp and the snake was hanging over a branch. We were drinking and chatting when one of us simply froze. He pointed to the snake. It was slithering down the tree and made off into the jungle! Vic looked decidedly pale . . .

That was not the only near escape. One night we came back to camp to find a tarantula catching moths in the lamplight outside our tent. A couple of hours later we were playing cards when a lizard fell from the trees onto our table and we all scattered, screaming like girls. I insisted on sleeping in a hammock for obvious reasons and one night I awoke knowing I wasn't alone! Underneath I saw a pair of eyes in the darkness. I just didn't want to know and I went back to sleep praying I'd wake up in the morning.

The jungle really was an experience in itself. The monkeys there sounded almost like a far-off high wind and the frogs sometimes were deafening, making almost bird-like calls. There were vampire bats everywhere, the weirdest of creatures, feeding off the bananas.

Eventually, we all decided that we had to admit defeat. We were running out of supplies and we just could not really catch the amount of bait that we required. In the end we simply had to give up and move out of our base back onto the river. Rather than face the complicated journey back to Quito, we found a small airstrip and after much haggling chartered a plane. Our plan was to move on to the coast to see if we could do a little bit of big game fishing. Even then, the trip had more in store for us for, as we flew high over the Andes, the engine became starved of oxygen and there were a few really shaky moments. On the coast, the members of the party fished really hard because we all wanted to go back with something. I caught a decent wahoo and one of us lost a blue marlin. The boats were around $250 a day which is very reasonable for a party and really some of the big game fishing there is out of this world. Apparently there is an island you can stay on as a base where the waters have hardly ever been fished.

I suppose in retrospect the trip was a failure, but then most prospecting journeys are. You really need to go out once just to get a hang of the place and then you can go again with ideas properly worked out. I want to go again because I hate to be beaten. Next time I will go in a party with two

Spanish speakers because that is really important. Very often we didn't really get our wishes through. I will also try and work out the bait problem. Quito market is full of small fish and if these could somehow be frozen and you could get them into the jungle there would be no more problems on that score. I think that Ecuador is a good base and certainly the people were very friendly and helpful and this is a major bonus. But location is the real problem and the real key. You must go when the water is low. To go when the water is twenty feet above normal is not giving yourself anything like a chance. In fact, some of our party returned six months after the original trip and found the river even higher, if at all possible. Needless to say, they didn't do any good at all. Location is the key, I again repeat. The idea is to actually see an arapaima. In fact, I would like to have men out there looking for them before I arrive. The rule then is to watch the fish, to work out its patrol route and place good baits well presented in front of it. It is fortunate that the arapaima is both huge and highly visible. Apparently, in good conditions it shows frequently above the surface and is absolutely unmistakable. Not having hooked an arapaima yet, I can't really say if our tackle would have been up to the job, but I suspect thirty or fifty class gear should be quite adequate for fish that probably grow to around three or four hundred pounds.

The whole scale of our problem is shown by the fact that in 1990 a ninety-pound arapaima was put forward as a world record. This is obviously a small specimen but it was caught on rod and line and therein lies the achievement. Mahseer are common by comparison! Even Goliath tigerfish are pretty thick on the ground.

Keith's story is a fascinating one in many respects and it shows that fish need not necessarily be caught to make an expedition very valuable. There is no doubt in my mind that arapaima are probably the most difficult freshwater fish to catch in the world and just talking to Keith on the banks of the Kennet one dull autumn day made me long for the adventure myself.

PART IV

African Journeys

Tigerfish

My father knew a man who travelled with a Mr Fox-Strangways who had fished all over the world and was even writing a book on the subject. When this man visited our house I was enthralled by him. He would spend the evening talking of great fish in distant lands and showing me a host of slides. Eventually a book arrived for me. Its title was *Wandering Fishermen* and our guest was the friend of its author Fox-Strangways. In its pages are some of the most dramatic encounters with tigerfish ever described.

The first tigerfish I ever saw took a 3/0 Silver Grey on a light gut cast. He was a beautiful creature and put up a wonderful fight; most astonishingly the cast was not bitten through, and we landed him, I regret to say, by kicking him ashore, which was a vandal's way of treating a stout-hearted fish. I am still a little ashamed of it, but the incident is for ever preserved in memory.

I was on a visit with a companion to Oguta Lake in southern Nigeria. The water looked wonderful, and we felt that we must do something about it; unfortunately we had nothing with us in the way of tackle except a few old salmon flies and casts which I used to carry around, in a rather nostalgic way, to cheer me up in that steaming country of flat, unrelieved bush and glaring sun. However, we borrowed a line and went out trolling from a canoe; we knew that the lake held crocodiles and were told it held fish, but at that time, as you will observe, we knew nothing about tigers.

We trolled and trolled, down to the junction of the lake with the Orashi river, back along the north shore, round and across, in deep water and shallow; never a touch. And then, just as we were about to turn in to the landing-place, disillusioned and dispirited, there was a magnificent snatch and up into the air astern of the canoe shot a flashing, silver shape, shaking its head furiously in the effort to dislodge the Silver Grey. We both yelled. Up went the fish again, and down again in a smash of spray; then up once more, savage, furious, with a wrench at the taut line that sent my heart into my mouth. This time my companion yelled. 'How do I stop him doing that?' he shouted, hanging on to the line like grim death; but meanwhile the fish had doubled and shot under the canoe. We disentangled the line with difficulty, almost helpless with excitement and laughter. The fish was tiring now. How to land him? We had no net, and

(page 135) *Andy Orme with one of his 100lb+ monsters*

feared for the hook-hold; it seemed better to try and beach him. The fishermen hopped out and ashore; but the fish had other ideas, and started thrashing in the shallows, and then, horrors! he gave a last feeble jump and threw the hook. For a moment he lay there, all three of us turned to stone; then somehow we managed to scoop and kick him ashore and he was ours.

And now, you will say, after all this fuss, how big was this magnificent fish? I will tell the truth; he weighed less than six pounds; but since then I have caught fish of ten times his weight that did not give me half the thrill he did.

Certainly the tiger is one of the most sporting, as well as the best-looking, of the fish to be found in the inland waters of Africa. You will meet him in most of the big river systems, and I do not think that his habits vary much, wherever he swims; I have caught him in the Niger and its tributaries and in the Zambezi and its feeders, and always he is the same, fast, fierce and unexpected, a compact, violent fish that takes like a thunderbolt and, unless you know your job, is gone like a flicker of light.

He is one of the Characinidae, and his proper name is *Hydrocynus*, and it seems that he may run to five different species. In Nigerian waters you will find him as *H. lineatus*, *H. forskalii*, and *H. brevis*; Northern Rhodesia calls him *lineatus*, and that is his name in the Nyasaland Shire, a tributary of the Zambezi. But in the Southern Rhodesian Zambezi, and in the Sabi and other rivers of that country he is known as *vittatus*, and this apparently, is his South African name too. It may well be that, in fact *lineatus* and *vittatus* are one and the same. *Forskalii* are found in the Nile system as well as in the Niger; and in the Congo and in Lake Tanganyika he lives in his giant form, the well named *H. goliath*.

Goliath must be a fellow worth looking at, but greatly to my regret I have never seen him and so cannot describe his appearance. The other species seem to be very much alike in looks, at any rate to the uninstructed angler's cursory survey, and I suspect that it is easy to make mistakes in classification. All are silver and fairly well streamlined, with dark horizontal lines on their bright sides, and fins and tail tipped or tinged with deep yellow or orange or sometimes orange-red. All have an adipose fin. The coloration of the fins seem to deepen as the fish grows bigger, and in an average ten-pounder the adipose fin will be scarlet or even dark crimson. All have the wicked, inter-locking teeth that help to give the fish its name, the powerful, scimitar-shaped fins and sickle tail, perfectly shaped for speed, and the head, which though blunter than in some other kinds of fast, predatory fish, yet gives the muscular body a perfect entry. The heavier specimens seem to be if anything less silvery than their smaller brothers, and to have a darker, more steel-blue tinge about their backs which the little ones do not show. But any tiger is a very fine fish; and if perhaps he does not possess quite the lovely symmetry of a spring salmon, or the speed and streamlining of a wahoo, or the endurance and blinding silver sheen of a bonefish, still he is a good-looker and a tough and wild fighter, his deep, narrow body perfectly adapted for sudden turns and accelerations and bursts of speed and every kind of aquabatics, and for a quite impressive range of aerobatics as well.

What weight do tigerfish attain? The answer seems to depend largely on the species concerned. As one might expect, the big *goliath* head the list, with specimens of seventy and eighty pounds from Lake Tanganyika; and I remember reading a good many years ago of a tigerfish of eighty-three pounds which was taken, as far as I recollect, in the Katanga province of the Belgian Congo and which must surely have been *goliath* too. *Lineatus* and the others do not seem to run so heavy. Southern Rhodesia has records of *lineatus* up to twenty-five pounds, with eighteen pounds as the rod-caught record: Northern Nigeria has a rod-caught specimen of twenty-four pounds, presumably a *lineatus*, taken at Katsina Ala in 1949. Southern Nigeria has had rod-caught *lineatus* up to at least eighteen pounds. In the Nyasaland Shire the rod-and-line record seems to stand at sixteen pounds. But in all these territories, the Africans will tell you that there are much bigger fish waiting to be caught; and maybe the Africans are right. Who knows? He is a poor-spirited sort of angler whose breast does not nourish hope eternal.

Tiger-fishing. What memories the words bring back! Wide, tropic rivers lying smooth as polished metal in the blazing sunshine, the gunwales of the canoe too hot to touch with comfort, the dural of your reel scorching, the sweat running out of your shirt sleeves and down your neck and into your eyes. The heat is terrific, and the glare off the water worse, and you are deeply thankful for the sissyfied dark glasses that the tough old African explorers never deigned to wear. You have trolled for hours, and never a touch, and you are bored with the whole show, and – Bang! your rod is pulled down flat, and the reel is screaming, and away, far away it seems astern of the canoe a great fish flashes out into the sunlight, thrashing frantically, and falls back with a smash of spray. Madly you reel up, to get the line tight again; and again the handles are dragged from your fingers by a savage, heavy run, and again up he comes, lashing and quivering with fury. Gradually you get him under control; the rushes are shorter now, the leaps less furious, until you have him close to the canoe, the hot sunlight shining through the brown water and lighting up his glimmering silver flanks and crimson fins and tail. He's done. And then, as you get the gaff ready, he plays the last card; from four feet down, that powerful tail shoots him up – up in a last defiant leap, flashing in the sunshine in a burst of glittering spray; you have a split-second glimpse of the spoon sailing past your head, and he is down again, sousing into the river with a wallowing splash. For an instant he lies there, almost within your reach, gasping, immobile, ten or twelve or fourteen pounds of first-class fighting fish; just for a long moment only, and then with a final flick of his strong, red-tipped tail he dives, and the river closes over him, and he is gone. That's tiger-fishing.

Or perhaps you are fishing a smaller, rockier river. You have dropped

A very old photograph of Fox-Strangways fishing for tigers; (right) *The man and his prize*

down from the cool uplands, past great plantations of eucalyptus with its shimmering, blue-grey leaves, past little settlements where flame trees and bouganvillea glow in the sunshine around the houses and where bauhinia and jacaranda are clouds of mauve and white and purple against the dark green of fir and indigenous forests; down the twisting, bumpy, escarpment road, through woods splashed and streaked with the bronze of young mombo leaves (it was the mombo which, in the old days before the introduction of textiles, gave Africans their bark-cloth) and the maroon and crimson and blood-red of lesser brachystegia; down, down two thousand feet to where arching bamboo and vivid, green, golden-flowered mtondo and scarlet-blossoming thorns stand out brilliantly against the parched greys and browns of the riverine plain.

It is swelteringly hot. Here, the river runs swiftly through rocky clefts and in racing, tumbling rapids; the banks are steep and piled with great boulders and choked with tall elephant grass; the water itself is deep and swirling, and dotted with islands of rock, on several of which sleepy-looking crocodiles are basking in the hot afternoon sunlight. High overhead, an eagle swings and circles, his wings now black in silhouette, now glinting with gold and chestnut as they catch the sun.

You thrust and clamber through dense bush and grass and tangling creepers, and over slippery rocks to where the river, penned into a narrow gorge, comes foaming through in a tremendous rush of roaring white water that gradually slackens into a rapid, and slows, and loses itself in the immense pool below. And from bank to bank a huge expanse of troubled, eddying water full of miniature whirlpools and sudden boils and unexplained disturbances; surely it might hold anything. All at once, just as when you get near a buffalo in the long grass your .375 Magnum feels like a .22 so now, as you look at the formidable pool, your hefty rod and stout wire trace seem quite a dainty outfit. The weight of water is tremendous; its sheer expanse will test your casting powers, and there are sly, subaqueous currents that will take your lure and give it a snatch as though a big fish had struck.

You scramble out on to a convenient rock and cast as far as you can over the foaming race at the throat of the pool. At once the stream snatches and straightens out your line; round comes the red and white feather, swooping and fluttering attractively, fifty yards below you and three feet under the surface of the grey-green water. Now it is just coming into the 'taking' area, where the deep eddying backwash curls round to meet the main current; careful now – Bang! you're into him. He comes straight out, five feet into the air, thrashing and shaking his head; then down again with a burst of spray, and almost before you can get your rod up properly he's away, slicing down and across the river, fast as a torpedo and with all that weight of water to help him. The reel screams. Wow! this is a fish! Up he

Fishing for tigers in the reedy swamps

comes, and out again, and this time you get a clearer view; he's a good one; might go twelve pounds. Now he turns and swims straight upstream towards you, the line bellying behind him; reel, reel, you must get the line tight or he'll be off; reel, your rod is in a hoop from the pull of the drowned line, reel madly; and at last, with a great sigh of relief, you feel him again. Another furious leap, and another; and now at length he is tiring; you catch a glimpse of him at the edge of the white water, fighting grimly away from you jagging and boring. Another jump and a flurry of spray; then the rod begins to tell, and you pull him in, in, still straining down and away with a stubborn savagery; now! the gaff goes in, and you stagger ashore with him over the slippery rocks, and slug him on the head till he lies quiet; and then, as you take out the hook, he gives a last kick and tries to bite. A gallant fish: he pulls down the balance to eleven pounds.

Your companion comes up, and you lay the fish out on a flat stone and admire his gleaming silver sides and the steel blue of his back and his orange and scarlet fins and tail. Behind you, the half-dozen diminutive African urchins who have attached themselves to the fishing party are chattering excitedly, and you catch snatches of the argument. 'My man got three!' 'Get away with you, my man got the biggest!' and so on; a good deal of small-boy pushing and shoving, and white teeth brilliant in impish black faces. Overhead the eagle is still circling majestically; across the water the crocodiles are still immobile on their chosen, sun-warmed rocks. And in that tumbling, grey-green water there must be more tigers; many of them bigger ones – what are you waiting for?

And that's tiger-fishing, too.

'The fiercest fish that swims' was L. J. McCormick's verdict on the tigerfish, a species that inspired him when he was in London and saw at Hardy's Tackle Shop the skull of an 8lb specimen. The armoury of diabolic teeth inspired him and the desire grew to know what fish could require such weapons. The dream was fulfilled, as he described in his book *Fishing Round the World*:

There was a considerable battle and though I could feel the fish was a small one, what a fighter! At last I got him to the canoe. He was a tigerfish all right, and, though he had the whole triangle of hooks in his mouth, I did not fancy him too much in the boat with those teeth.

The tigerfish is different from most fish, in as much as it has long fearfully sharp teeth fixed like a bear trap on the outside of its mouth, there being slots in the lips to allow the teeth, when the mouth is closed, to remain on the exterior in a glittering menace. This gives to its face a devilish expression which can be well appreciated at close range. Apart from this, it is one of the most beautiful fish. Made like a very stocky salmon, it is covered with large, bright scales. In this fish they were a pale lemon colour. Along the body ran darker scales in stripes and it is from this circumstance, no doubt, that it has received its English name. The fins were all of brilliant orange.

McCormick suffered many disappointments in Africa, as well as dangers, but one of the deepest frustrations was the fact that it was almost impossible to set the hooks into the tigerfish's mouth.

I counted once sixteen strikes before the hook stayed in, and this was by no means an abnormal ratio. Generally the fish would clamp down firmly on the spoon but with all my strength I could not drive the hook home, while deep scratches were scored on the tough metal by their teeth. I tried every kind of hook and bait and finally at the head of the spoon, I added a triangle hook, so that if a tigerfish took hold at all it must get a barb in its mouth. My best fish, an eighteen-and-a-half pounder, was caught with this new armament; in fact it was obtained with my first cast after I had gone to all the trouble of wiring on the extra hook in that blistering heat. I had lost so many fish by that time that I felt sure this one would get off too, but he did not. He was in marvellous condition and was in such a hurry to go downstream that it was all I could do to stop him. In the excitement I

Jim Deterding with a small but perfectly shaped tigerfish

Tigerfish bay!

The locals can often do the job more thoroughly!

almost lost my hat and my balance as well. The fish did not quite know whether it was better to shake the hook out in the air or to pull me in and swallow me. I've never seen a finer exhibition of jumping or experienced a fiercer strain on my line for so small a fish.

Modern anglers still search for tigerfish and one of them, Paul Boote, has taken the quest a stage further and hunted the tigerfish's enormous cousin, the Goliath. Paul's journey in the Congo Basin is one of the great achievements of modern angling history. Yet it is easy to see what so inspired Paul who risked his life searching for the Goliath. Its amazing teeth are probably its most outstanding feature and in a specimen of 40 or 50lb may be 1¼in long and ⁴/₁₀in wide at the base. And 80-pounders have been caught in the distant past with sightings of fish that could have weighed as much as a 100–125lb. It is in every way a ferocious fish and its feeding furies are phenomenal. Sometimes its pursuit of prey-fish is so frantic that it will beach itself with its final lunge. It is well known for smaller Goliaths of, say, 20–30lb to be seized by much bigger fish as they are being played and, even more extraordinary, giant Goliath tigerfish have head-butted the boats from which anglers have fished. Yes, the Goliath tigerfish inhabit a savage world:

> The River Congo is no place for an animal with a weak heart. The four important cohabitants are crocodiles, Nile perch, and the two varieties of tigerfish. Each of these is possessed of an insatiable craving to devour their own kind as well as the others. Doctor Gillet is convinced that tigerfish gobble up young crocodiles with the greatest zest and crocodiles certainly return the compliment. The Nile perch helps itself to both, and is itself the victim of the others. Thus we have a perfect example of a neutral devouration society – a state of affairs which probably accounts for the comparatively small number of Goliaths that reach full maturity.
>
> (*Game Fish of the World*, Ed. Brian Vesey-Fitzgerald)

The Goliath is equally ferocious when it comes to human beings and natives claim that it attacks them when swimming and shows a liking for biting off their genitals. The same Doctor Gillet mentioned above personally claimed to have cared for three natives who were wounded by Goliaths. The first of these was a water-carrier whose left hand had been seized while he was leaning out of his canoe to wash. He lost four fingers that were severed completely from his palm as if they had been cut off by an axe. The other two cases were of native boys, one of whom had a piece torn out of his back, while the other was severely bitten on the thigh.

Nile Perch

The Nile perch is a member of the family of giant perch that are found in various rivers throughout the world. It is a colossal fish and can grow to well in excess of 200lb, although a 100lb fish is a magnificent prize and is seen as the catch of a lifetime. Their size is complemented by their looks. Freshly caught, under the tropical sun, they flash blues and silvers back at the exotic world they inhabit. Several anglers have spoken of the awe that they have felt upon seeing the great sheet of silver rise towards their boat from the depths and the gasps that they have let out when the fish's great back has burst up towards the sun.

There is, however, a drawback. Most of Nile perch fishing carried out today is on the huge waters of Lake Victoria. There can be no doubt that today trolling under the guidance of an expert boatman is an experience to remember. Hits to the big lures are frequent, savage and rod-wrenching, and Andy Orme has even had his rods snapped at the butt by the ferocity of the take. Such sights do not happen in every angler's lifetime. However, this type of fishing is somewhat mechanical: success largely depends on the knowledge of the boatman rather than on any skill on the angler's part. Even when these leviathans are hooked, their fight tends to be heavy and sluggish rather than dramatic or inspiring. Perhaps it is the heat of the water that dulls the fight and means that most hooked Nile perch, even the large ones, are landed Nile perch. All in all, a staggering catch of Nile perch from Lake Victoria is not seen as a massive angling achievement but rather as a fun experience for those who are privileged enough to enjoy it. This, however, is not to decry all Nile perch adventures.

Andy Orme certainly deserves his place in this book. A pre-booked tourist trip was not for him, but rather he flew direct into Mombasa, Kenya's second city and a major port, where he hired a Suzuki jeep and prepared to drive himself deep into Kenya. The road north-west was a difficult one. Early rains had left the tracks treacherous and frequently the small jeep appeared ready to founder. The game viewing throughout was magnificent but there was always the nagging fear of breakdown which could have proved disastrous for a man travelling alone with no back-up.

For a while Andy fished on Lake Naivasha which is a lovely freshwater lake in Kenya's Rift Valley. Here he stayed in a hut on the lake shore, hired a rowing-boat and caught many small but energetic bass. Both scenery and wildlife were extraordinary but the legendary perch of Lake Victoria pulled him further into the country.

Eventually he arrived at Kisumu, which is situated on a bay on Lake Victoria. Here the fisheries officer told him to travel on to Homa Bay and to Rusinga Island. Heavy rain followed Andy all the way and the driving became treacherous.

By now Andy was exhausted, so he rested in a room at the local insect research station. Further enquiries revealed a lodge on Rusinga Island itself and he confirmed a room and set off once more. At last he had arrived on

An historic photograph of a Nile perch taken around the turn of the century. Note the massive centrepin used to catch the fish

A heart-stopping moment in Andy Orme's journey

Lake Victoria after a journey of hundreds of miles through game reserves and vast deserted plains. That night, despite his tiredness, excitement kept him awake and he was up before dawn checking the gear as all fanatical fishermen will. At first light he was away, guided by his boatman towards some distant islands. Lures were trolled on 30lb line attached to 2lb test curve carp rods and by 8 o'clock the sun was blistering.

Over the next two days Andy experienced angling that made the journey more than worth the effort. The first day saw him catch 11 fish: including one double, one 20-pounder, three 30-pounders, two 40-pounders, two 50-pounders, a 60-pounder and a monster which weighed just over 100lb, and all these fish came in just one morning. The second day started just as well and soon 14 fish of 50lb were landed.

However, the memory of the 100-pounder from the previous day haunted him and he wished for just one more monster before the journey back to civilisation. Soon it was midday and time to return to the lodge. However, John the boatman suggested one last troll over a fabled area. Once again Andy's courage was rewarded when a huge fish took the lure. The fight lasted for over fifteen minutes in burning sun, but at last they saw a massive sheet of silver rising to the surface. Ten more minutes elapsed before the fish

Shirley Deterding has fished successfully for years

was finally brought to the surface next to the boat and Andy had caught another 100lb Nile perch.

The drive back from Victoria to Mombasa was even more hazardous than the drive in. Andy became lost in reserves and found himself way off made-up roads. He began to fear for his very safety when he found himself in prohibited areas and surrounded by gangs of armed men. There was a lot of luck as well as judgement attached to his return to the city and Andy himself admits that the journey was to a large extent a foolhardy one and one that it would be foolish to recommend to others. Still, the fact remains that it was completed successfully and provided Andy with wonderful memories.

Perhaps Nile perch are always a source of adventure for anglers. Shirley Deterding's experience with them was certainly fraught with danger.

On our many trips to Kenya, Jim, my husband, and I have always tried to get up to Lake Rudolph, or Turkana as it is now called – a remote and very dramatic inland sea over two hundred miles long, stretching into Ethiopia. This is a most extraordinary area and is exceedingly hot and dry. The distant mountains and the surrounding desert make it seem like a lunar landscape and the hot high winds blow constantly down the valley. There is little vegetation apart from scrub and the occasional palm tree and to stay there for more than four or five days is more than an ordeal.

There are two fishing lodges on the lake but we elected to fly our small plane on to an island in the lake – simply a tiny mound in the middle of miles of saline water. The landing was hair-raising and we were lucky to touch down on what was little more than an uphill clearing. We set up camp under a thorn-bush with just a tarpaulin thrown over to keep the burning sun off. We had an inflatable boat with us and a few basic rations plus our fishing tackle. We had to clear the crocodiles from the beach before we could even think of fishing. Nile perch was our aim, the prehistoric-looking fish with the huge head and the magnificent silver body. Immediately we began to catch fish that were all returned, apart from those that we were to eat for dinner. This was one of those occasions when we had to fish to live.

The crocodiles continued to swarm around the island and we constantly had to throw stones at them if we wanted either to bathe or fish, and it was hard to prevent them from eating the fish that we caught – or, come to that, from eating us!

On the second day we went round to the end of the island, catching fish as we went and found a feeding shoal of tilapia. Around this shoal where their predators, also in a feeding frenzy, the Nile perch and the crocodiles. We hooked fish at almost every cast, some big ones, but then I was into something that exceeded all expectations. The fight went on and on under the burning sun and at times it actually towed our boat in circles away from the shore. In the end, I managed to bring it along-side and lift the head clear and the fish was simply enormous. The guide judged it to be over two hundred pounds and it was far too large to even consider boating. I gladly unhooked it as it floated by us and released this giant prehistoric fish into the depths where hopefully it will live for many years to come.

It was after this fish that we decided to do something which now seems incredibly stupid. We planned to make a trip to the legendary Murchison Falls, over the border in Uganda, where the perch are fabled for their size and fighting ability. To say it was dangerous to attempt this flight is an understatement. General Amin's troops still ranged freely in the desert, killing all before them with no questions asked. Every building around the falls had been raized to the ground, we were told. However, we set off with our tiny plane loaded with as many cans of aviation fuel as we could carry. The weight of these was terrific and we had to pare down our stores to an absolute minimum or the plane would never have lifted off. We refuelled at Lake Victoria, telling the authorities that we were on our way to Lake Turkana. Then we flew low to avoid showing on the radar and crossed the border into Uganda, flying up the long winding River Nile which flows across country from Kenya.

The realisation grew that I was an illegal immigrant with no passport and no official permission to enter the country. The possibility of a life in Idi Amin's jails began to raise a very ugly head. However, we landed on a strip where a couple of derelict planes lay forlornly on their sides and where no one else was in sight. We pushed our plane to the side of the runway and made it secure to some large stones and then unloaded the gear and carried it down to the water's edge. Eventually, a couple of natives appeared with a small boat and after bargaining a price we set off up-river piled high with our stores and equipment. It was a peaceful trip, with the bird life, hippos and crocodiles quietly enjoying their day along the banks. Then we heard the roar of the falls! They were a sight I will never forget! We unloaded our equipment on to a beach down-stream of the magnificent wall of water and set up our rods ready for immediate fishing. We began close to the falls themselves and soon were catching fish in the foaming water. It was exhilarating sport and again we just kept what we required for our food.

As the sun began to sink I was fighting a huge fish which tore off downstream so quickly it was impossible for me to follow. The battle raged, but at last, with aching arms, I began to get a little line back on to the reel. It was then that everything stopped dead. After a pause the line started to go again, steadily and slowly with no stopping until it simply snapped off at the empty reel drum. I shook my head in disbelief and as I did so a roar of water erupted two hundred yards from me. A crocodile had surfaced, shaking its massive head, and in its jaws was lodged a sixty pound Nile perch, no doubt with my spinner still in its mouth.

We were marooned in this wonderful place for five days and we ran out of all our stores and drinks. Nile perch became the only ration and at last we even ran out of fresh water. Thank God for our two little Jack Russell terriers that had come with us and which kept the crocodiles at bay all night. Sadly, for them too, it was Nile perch, morning and night. This really was a journey I will always remember . . . and will never repeat!

Linda and Jim Tyree with colossal perch of 154lb, 123lb and 112lb – a staggering shot